DOWN FROM THE IVORY TOWER

DOWN FROM THE IVORY TOWER

8 sessions on living our theology from Romans 1–8

by John M. Dettoni

A DIVISION OF SCRIPTURE PRESS PUBLICATIONS INC.
USA CANADA ENGLAND

Most Scripture quotations are from the *Holy Bible, New International Version®.* Copyright © 1973, 1978, 1984 by International Bible Society. Used by permission of Zondervan Publishing House. All rights reserved.

Recommended Dewey Decimal Classification: 227.1
Suggested Subject Heading: EPISTLES: ROMANS

Library of Congress Catalog Card Number: 93-50844
ISBN: 1-56476-323-4

1 2 3 4 5 6 7 8 9 10   Printing / Year   97 96 95 94 93

© 1994 by SP Publications, Inc. All rights reserved. Printed in the United States of America. No part of this book may be reproduced without written permission, except for brief quotations in books, critical articles, and reviews.

VICTOR BOOKS
A division of SP Publications, Inc.
　　　Wheaton, Illinois 60187

CONTENTS

PURPOSE: To develop a theology that will guide not only our thinking, but our living.

INTRODUCTION	7
IS THIS YOUR FIRST SMALL GROUP?	9
SESSION 1 – LIVING BY FAITH Romans 1:1-17	13
SESSION 2 – FIRST THE BAD NEWS Romans 1:18-32	21
SESSION 3 – GUILTY OR NOT GUILTY? Romans 3:9-31	33
SESSION 4 – MODEL STUDENTS Romans 4:1-25	41
SESSION 5 – PEACE AND JOY IN LIFE'S UPS AND DOWNS Romans 5:1-5	51
SESSION 6 – NEW LIFE Romans 6:1-14; 7:21-25	59
SESSION 7 – SOS Romans 8:1-17	69
SESSION 8 – NEVER ABANDONED; ALWAYS LOVED Romans 8:28-39	81
DEAR SMALL GROUP LEADER	90
LEADER'S GUIDE	92

INTRODUCTION

Down from the Ivory Tower is for people who want to build a livable theology that answers the "so what?" questions of life. An in-depth Leader's Guide is included at the back of the book with suggested time guidelines to help you structure your emphases. Each of the 8 sessions contains the following elements:

❏ **Getting Acquainted**—activities or selected readings to help you begin thinking and sharing from your life and experiences about the subject of the session. Use only those options that seem appropriate for your group.

❏ **Gaining Insight**—questions and in-depth Bible study to help you gain principles from Scripture for life-related application.

❏ **Growing by Doing**—an opportunity to practice the truth learned in the Gaining Insight section.

❏ **Going the Second Mile**—a personal enrichment section for you to do on your own.

❏ **Session Objectives**—goals listed in the Leader's Guide that describe what should happen in the group by the end of the session.

IS THIS YOUR FIRST SMALL GROUP?

'smol grüp: A limited number of individuals assembled together having some unifying relationship.

Kris'chen 'smol grüp: 4–12 persons who meet together on a regular basis, over a determined period of time, for the shared purpose of pursuing biblical truth. They seek to mature in Christ and become equipped to serve as His ministers in the world.

Picture Your First Small Group.

List some words that describe what you want your small group to look like.

What Kind Of Small Group Do You Have?

People form all kinds of groups based on gender, age, marital status, and so forth. There are advantages and disadvantages to each. Here are just a few:

❑ **Same Age Groups** will probably share similar needs and interests.

- **Intergenerational Groups** bring together people with different perspectives and life experiences.

- **Men's or Women's Groups** usually allow greater freedom in sharing and deal with more focused topics.

- **Singles or Married Groups** determine their relationship emphases based on the needs of a particular marital status.

- **Mixed Gender Groups (singles and/or couples)** stimulate interaction and broaden viewpoints while reflecting varied lifestyles.

However, the most important area of "alikeness" to consider when forming a group is an **agreed-on purpose.** Differences in purpose will sabotage your group and keep its members from bonding. If, for example, Mark wants to pray but not play while Jan's goal is to learn through playing, then Mark and Jan's group will probably not go anywhere. People need different groups at different times in their lives. Some groups will focus on sharing and accountability, some on work projects or service, and others on worship. *Your small group must be made up of persons who have similar goals.*

How Big Should Your Small Group Be?
The **fewest** people to include would be **4**. Accountability will be high, but absenteeism may become a problem.

The **most** to include would be **12**. But you will need to subdivide regularly into groups of 3 or 4 if you want people to feel cared for and to have time for sharing.

How Long Should You Meet?
8 Weeks gives you a start toward becoming a close community, but doesn't overburden busy schedules. Count on needing three or four weeks to develop a significant trust level. The smaller the group, the more quickly trust develops.

Weekly Meetings will establish bonding at a good pace and allow for accountability. The least you can meet and still be an effective group is once a month. If you choose the latter, work at individual contact among group members between meetings.

You will need **75 minutes** to accomplish a quality meeting. The larger the size, the more time it takes to become a healthy group. Serving refreshments will add 20–30 minutes, and singing and/or prayer time, another 20–30 minutes. Your time duration may be determined by the time of day you meet and by the amount of energy members bring to the group. Better to start small and ask for more time when it is needed because of growth.

What Will Your Group Do?
To be effective, each small group meeting should include:

1. **Sharing**—You need to share who you are and what is happening in your life. This serves as a basis for relationship building and becomes a springboard for searching out scriptural truth.

2. **Scripture**—There must always be biblical input from the Lord to teach, rebuke, correct, and train in right living. Such material serves to move your group in the direction of maturity in Christ and protects from pooled ignorance and distorted introspection.

3. **Truth in practice**—It is vital to provide opportunities for *doing* the Word of God. Experiencing this within the group insures greater likelihood that insights gained will be utilized in everyday living.

Other elements your group may wish to add to these three are: a time of **worship, specific prayer** for group members, **shared projects**, a time to **socialize** and enjoy **refreshments**, and **recreation.**

ONE

Living by Faith

Doing Theology

"I don't have a theology." True or false? False! We all have a theology. It may not be very well expressed; it may be incipient or hardly even stated. But when push comes to shove in our thinking about God and His actions, or when we talk to others—our children, our friends, our relatives—about why God seems to have acted in a certain way, we have to give a theological answer, even if it is not a good one. We give our thoughts on the issues. And these thoughts are our basic, though perhaps simple, attempts to "do theology."

We often think theology is some esoteric thinking that only the most intellectual, academic, and inspired people can do. I must admit that my image of theologians is not very positive: a group of old men, sitting around a dusty, book-strewn room, in the dim light from the leaded windows of a cloister. Those men sit, talking a language that I recognize—it's my native language—but in words that I could never understand. Right now, I see them still debating how many angels can dance on the head of a pin.

Are theologians really like that? Some undoubtedly are. But not all theologians are "professionals" who theologize for a living. In this study of Romans, we will all become junior theologians, theologians in our own right as we think Paul's thoughts after him. But we will not fall into the trap that limits so many theologians and theological statements. We will not just think! We will reflect and use our minds, of course, but we will also ask the "So what?" question. If certain things are true about God, the world, sin, righteousness, etc., then what differences do they make in our lives?

The challenge to us is to think, to ask "So what?" questions, to commit ourselves to what the Holy Spirit is saying to us and begin to be transformed more and more into the likeness of Jesus Christ.

GETTING ACQUAINTED

Portrait of a Theologian
What do you think of when you hear the words *theology* and *theologian*? Sketch a portrait of a theologian here (or jot down descriptive words or phrases, if you prefer).

- highly intelligent
- suit n' tie kinda guy
- briefcase
- pop bottle glasses
- pens in pocket

- ❏ Would your imaginary theologian be interesting to talk to? Possible
- ❏ Would you feel secure talking with him or her? Doubt it.
- ❏ Do you know anyone whom you might classify as a theologian? Pastor Drennan
- ❏ What is that person like?

Now imagine you could talk with the Apostle Paul.
- ❏ What do you think he would be like compared with the theologians that you've just described? How would he be different? The same?
- ❏ Would you be able to talk and ask Paul questions?
- ❏ Do you think he would be helpful to you as you tried to become more Christlike in your daily Christian life? Why or why not?

LIVING BY FAITH

Good News
Think of some personal, really good news that you've heard recently. How excited were you to hear it? Share that good news with your group. Describe how you felt when you heard it. As each group member shares his/her good news, see if there are any similar responses to that good news. List the similarities.

Good NEWS: Exsemtion from COMM 1000.
- *felt relieved*
- *honoured to be asked to Tutor.*

GAINING INSIGHT

Faith and Gospel
Write a definition of faith. Share your definition with the rest of the group.

- *belief in something/someone unseen.*
- *trust in the unknowing.*

Read Romans 1:1-17.

¹Paul, a servant of Christ Jesus, called to be an apostle and set apart for the Gospel of God—²the Gospel He promised beforehand through His prophets in the Holy Scriptures ³regarding His Son, who as to His human nature was a descendant of David, ⁴and who through the Spirit of holiness was declared with power to be the Son of God by His resurrection from the dead: Jesus Christ our Lord. ⁵Through Him and for His name's sake, we received grace and apostleship to call people from among all the Gentiles to the obedience that comes from faith. ⁶And you also are among those who are called to belong to Jesus Christ.

⁷To all in Rome who are loved by God and called to be saints:

Grace and peace to you from God our Father and from the Lord Jesus Christ.

⁸First, I thank my God through Jesus Christ for all of you, because your faith is being reported all over the world. ⁹God, whom I serve with my whole heart in preaching the Gospel of His Son, is my witness how constantly I remember you ¹⁰in my prayers at all times; and I pray that now at last by God's will the way may be opened for me to come to you.

¹¹I long to see you so that I may impart to you some spiritual gift to make you strong—¹²that is, that you and I may be mutually encouraged by each other's faith. ¹³I do not want you to be unaware, brothers, that I planned many times to come to you (but have been prevented from doing so until now) in order that I might have a harvest among you, just as I have had among the other Gentiles.

¹⁴I am obligated both to Greeks and non-Greeks, both to the wise and the foolish. ¹⁵That is why I am so eager to preach the Gospel also to you who are at Rome.

¹⁶I am not ashamed of the Gospel, because it is the power of God for the salvation of everyone who believes: first for the Jew, then for the Gentile. ¹⁷For in the Gospel a righteousness from God is revealed, a righteousness that is by faith from first to last, just as it is written: "The righteous will live by faith."

Romans 1:1-17

Divide into two groups.

Group one should reread Romans 1:1-17, looking for all references to the Gospel—its character, who is its source, who owns it, what its content is—anything that Paul uses to describe the Gospel.

Group two should also reread Romans 1:1-17, observing all references to faith and belief—its content, who believes, for whom faith is necessary, the results of faith.

LIVING BY FAITH

Use the space below to write your observations.

Share with the whole group the findings of each of the two groups. Add significant observations to your own list from those shared by the rest of your group.

What is the relationship between the Gospel and faith? Try by yourself to write two sentences that show how the Gospel and faith relate to each other, then share your summary with the group.

Without out the Gospel we wouldn't be able to support our faith.

Responding and Receiving
Look again at Romans 1:1-17. Summarize what it says by completing the following chart.

GOD'S ACTIONS	OUR RESPONSE	GOD IN US
promised the Gospel	obedience	service encouraging others.

The Gospel can be received only by faith or belief (v. 1) in its message and the Person that it is about. Now is the time to refine our definition of faith. As a whole group, let's review the definitions we wrote individually and try to decide on one fairly complete definition for the whole group.

GROWING BY DOING

Faith-less vs. Faith-full
It is clear that faith is not just something that one does once and then forgets about. In fact, the opposite is true: "The righteous will live [day by day] by faith" (v. 17). Now is the time to focus on that daily living by faith.

In groups of two, determine how to demonstrate to the entire group how in one typical area of our lives we do not live by faith. Demonstrate this to your whole group.

Reassemble in your groups of two and determine how to show the same area of life as it would look if you walked by faith.

Hot Spots
If you were to live by faith each moment of the day, what two or three things would be affected in your life? Consider things like nervousness, fretfulness, anxiety, worry, over-controlling yourself and/or others, being a "workaholic," etc. List these in the space below.

- worrying
- insecurities

Now, to the degree the items on your list are not too personal, share these with the whole group. Note the various areas of life that the group focused upon. And modify your own list as appropriate.

Close in prayer that God will enable you to walk by faith in each area that you chose. Do this either in pairs or as a circle prayer with the whole group.

GOING THE SECOND MILE

Sharing Support

Choose one or two items from the list that you just wrote which you would like to change this week. Write or circle those on your list. If you feel comfortable, share that list with others in your group or with a group member. Ask one person to call you at about halfway through the week to see how you are doing in your faith walk this week. You should also call someone from the group and ask the same question. Be sure you know who is calling whom.

TWO

First the Bad News

Bad News

Bad news travels fast, so the saying goes. When you read today's paper or watched the TV news or listened to the radio, was the news predominantly good or bad? Most of us recall a barrage of bad news: murders, robberies, rapes, drive-by shootings, arrests for various crimes, natural disasters, international terrorism, ethnic battles. The good news is hardly ever highlighted. When it is, it is usually done with an introduction like this: "We've reported an awful lot of bad news, but we have one piece of good news. . . ." One piece of good news is suppose to salve the 21 minutes of bad news.

Paul the Apostle is like a TV news reporter. He has about two and a half chapters of really bad news, culminating in Romans 3:10-11. We will look first at Romans 1:18-32 in order to determine why God is justifiably angry at humanity. In next week's session we will take one last look at humanity's sinful case before we move on to the really Good News of faith in Christ.

DOWN FROM THE IVORY TOWER

GETTING ACQUAINTED

What Have You Heard?
Bad news is everywhere.

- What bad news have you heard in the last 24 hours (assuming that it is not so horrible that you do not want to talk about it)? Briercrest Teacher's deaths
- How did it make you feel? Sad, Confused,
- Is there anything that you can do after the fact to change the bad news into good news? Why or why not? No,

All the News That's Fit to Print
Your group facilitator has brought the front section of the last several days of a local newspaper. Look at the front pages.

- How many stories are about good news?
- How many stories are about bad news?
- Why is it that bad-news stories usually outnumber the good?

GAINING INSIGHT

Downwardly Mobile
Paul, like our contemporary news reporters, has a significant amount of bad news to tell his readers. Read aloud Romans 1:18-32.

[18]The wrath of God is being revealed from heaven against all the godlessness and wickedness of men who suppress the truth by their wickedness, [19]since what may be known about God is plain to them, because God has made it plain to them. [20]For since the creation of the world, God's invisible qualities—His eternal power and divine nature—have been clearly seen, being understood from what has been made, so that men are without excuse.

[21]For although they knew God, they neither glorified Him as God nor gave thanks to Him, but their thinking became futile and their foolish hearts were darkened. [22]Although they claimed to be wise, they became fools [23]and exchanged the glory of the immortal God for images made

to look like mortal man and birds and animals and reptiles.

²⁴Therefore God gave them over in the sinful desires of their hearts to sexual impurity for the degrading of their bodies with one another. ²⁵They exchanged the truth of God for a lie, and worshiped and served created things rather than the Creator—who is forever praised. Amen.

²⁶Because of this, God gave them over to shameful lusts. Even their women exchanged natural relations for unnatural ones. ²⁷In the same way the men also abandoned natural relations with women and were inflamed with lust for one another. Men committed indecent acts with other men, and received in themselves the due penalty for their perversion.

²⁸Furthermore, since they did not think it worthwhile to retain the knowledge of God, He gave them over to a depraved mind, to do what ought not to be done. ²⁹They have become filled with every kind of wickedness, evil, greed and depravity. They are full of envy, murder, strife, deceit and malice. They are gossips, ³⁰slanderers, God-haters, insolent, arrogant and boastful; they invent ways of doing evil; they disobey their parents; ³¹they are senseless, faithless, heartless, ruthless. ³²Although they know God's righteous decree that those who do such things deserve death, they not only continue to do these very things but also approve of those who practice them.

Romans 1:18-32

List the various sins that Paul mentions.

Notice the crescendo of accusations by God and responses from God. Notice the continual downward spiral of humanity. Not a pretty picture.

Then and Now

Your group leader has some popular magazines on hand. Look through the magazines and tear out pictures of any of the sins that Paul mentioned in Romans 1:18-32 and any other sins that you see in the pictures. Paste them on the paper that your group facilitator has brought.

Now stand back and look at the pictures of sin that you found in the magazines. Does Paul mention any sins you did not find in contemporary print?

What might be the reason for any omissions?

What other sins did you find that Paul did not mention?

Are these "new" sins or did Paul just omit them from his list?

In a sentence, what is your response to the pictures of sin that you found? Write your thoughts below and share them with your group.

Cause and Effect

As you read what Paul has said about humanity's sins, what is the basic sin of humanity? What is its root cause? Write down your thoughts. Share what you have written with the person to either side of you.

Reread the passage. Fill in the effects of sin on the relationships listed in the three columns of this chart.

RELATIONSHIPS WITH GOD	RELATIONSHIPS WITH SELF	RELATIONSHIPS WITH OTHERS

What are the connections between the three columns?

Reread verses 18, 24, 26, and 28.

¹⁸The wrath of God is being revealed from heaven against all the godlessness and wickedness of men who suppress the truth by their wickedness.... ²⁴Therefore God gave them over in the sinful desires of their hearts to sexual impurity for the degrading of their bodies with one another.... ²⁶Because of this, God gave them over to shameful lusts. Even their women exchanged natural relations for unnatural ones.... ²⁸Furthermore, since they did not think it worthwhile to retain the knowledge of God, He gave them over to a depraved mind, to do what ought not to be done.

Romans 1:18, 24, 26, 28

What are some results of humanity's sins?

Notice the common phrase in these verses. What do you think that phrase means?

What is the progression of the sins that Paul states?

When you read and think about what Paul is saying about humanity and our sins, what feelings do you have? Close your eyes for a minute and imagine what it would be like to have God give you over to your most egocentric, selfish, passion-driven sins. Try to express to your group some of what you felt when you did this.

GROWING BY DOING

Rate Your Reaction
Look at the lists of sins that you have compiled above. Do you know anyone who does any of these sins? Just in case you run in fairly "good" moral circles, look at verses 29 and 30 where the more subtle sins of greed, envy, deceit, malice, gossip, and boasting are mentioned. Perhaps your friends, relatives, coworkers, and neighbors are not involved in what we often called "gross sins," but there is probably no one who has not been guilty of one of these more subtle but just as destructive sins.

Toward which kinds of sins are you most likely to feel great repulsion?

Which ones are you less repulsed by? Why?

Of the two classes of sins in this chapter, gross and subtle, which ones do you find yourself doing? Is there any connection between your kind of sin and your response to that kind of sin?

Why do we often classify sins according to how gross or externally immoral they are? Why do we not feel the same revulsion to the more "genteel sins"?

It is easy to combine sin and sinners and to hate both. If that were the case, God would never have sent Christ to die for our sins. As Paul says in Romans 5:8, "But God demonstrates His own love for us in this: While we were still sinners, Christ died for us."

How do you feel about people who do the things listed in Romans 1:18-32? Do you feel revulsion? Do some of those sins "make your skin crawl" in abhorrence? It is one thing to abhor sin; it is quite another to abhor the sinner. Christ never died to bring "good sinners" to God. There is no such person as a "good sinner." Christ died for sinners.

Examine Yourself

We have been discussing classifications of sins and our responses to sin and sinners. Now think for a minute about sin in your own life. (It is rather unpopular in our day and age to speak about sin, but we can hardly overlook it when Paul focuses so sharply on it in chapters one, two, and three of Romans.) As you review the list of sins in this chapter one more time, remember Christ's words:

[21]You have heard that it was said to the people long ago, "Do not murder, and anyone who murders will be subject to judgment." [22]But I tell you that anyone who is angry with his brother will be subject to judgment.

[27]You have heard that it was said, "Do not commit adultery." [28]But I tell you that anyone who looks at a woman lustfully has already committed adultery with her in his heart.

[33]Again, you have heard that it was said to the people long ago, "Do not break your oath, but keep the oaths you have made to the Lord." [34]But I tell you, Do not swear at all: either by heaven, for it is God's throne; [35]or by the earth, for it is His footstool; or by Jerusalem, for it is the city of the Great King. [36]And do not swear by your head, for you cannot make even one hair white or black. [37]Simply let your "Yes" be "Yes," and your "No," "No"; anything beyond this comes from the evil one.
                              Matthew 5:21-22; 27-28; 33-37

One murders in one's heart when one hates his brother; one commits adultery by lust and not just by sexual intercourse; one uses God's name in vain by taking an oath. It is not just the act that causes sin; it is the thought that precedes it. With this in mind then, what sins do you identify with in this chapter? Take a minute or so to think silently about the list as it applies to your own life now.

As you look at the sins that you see in your life, which can you identify as having to do with taking control of your own destiny apart from God's Word? Place a check mark next to the one or ones that are control-issue sins.

Now look at those check-marked sins. What observation can you make about those sins? Why is control the major issue? What can you do to change this? List two or three things that you could do, with God's help, to change any one of those you checked.

Respond to God
One response to seeing the sins of humanity in general and our own in particular could be despair. What a hopeless mess we people are in! But God does not want us to lose hope. Just the opposite. Our sin should bring us to a state of gratitude for being forgiven. How does God's Good News rescue us from despair and hopelessness and give us new life? Jot down a few ideas. Share your observations with your group.

Write a short prayer thanking God for the forgiveness of your sins and for the possibility of allowing Him to control your life. If you are willing to share it with the group, read it aloud for others to add their own "Amen."

GOING THE SECOND MILE

Releasing Control
Control of one's life is a constant issue for Christians and non-Christians alike. The first steps in the Twelve Step pro-

gram for Alcoholics Anonymous (AA) are to realize that one cannot overcome temptation (sin) on one's own and that a "higher power" is needed. As Christians, we constantly need to be grounded in allowing God to control us rather than attempting to control God. We often think of God as our genie in our little lamp, much like Aladdin and his magic lamp. We want to rub the lamp and have God pop out, asking how He can serve us next. God does not take the posture of slave to our desires or even our needs. He remains always the Sovereign Lord, quite independent of our commands.

This week, continue to work on the major sin(s) that you checked above. Here are three things you can do:

- ❑ Pray each morning and throughout the day that God, not you yourself, will control you. Give yourself reminders throughout the day to pray by writing stick-on notes to yourself and placing them in strategic places throughout your house, car, office, place of work—wherever you will

- ❑ see them and be reminded. The notes do not have to announce your sin to any who see them. Just a cryptic "Remember" or "Pray" will remind you to pray.

- ❑ Ask someone from your group to pray every day for you, and commit to pray for him or her, too. The commitment to pray is a significant covenant.

- ❑ Call the other person at least twice in the next seven days to remind him or her that you are praying, let him or her know how you yourself are doing, and ask how you can pray more intelligently for him or her. NOTE: You do not need to ask how well that person is overcoming the sin that you were praying about. If he or she wants you to know, you will be told. All you need to know is that the person is finding the spiritual strength necessary or needs more prayer and encouragement to overcome that particular sin.

THREE

Guilty or Not Guilty?

Good and Guilty

A man I knew, before he became a Christian late in his life, used to say that his good deeds were far better than many other people's. God certainly would reward him. If not, he'd be in hell with all his good friends and they would have a very long card game! Somehow he did not quite have the right picture of God, sin, his good works, and hell. He had plenty of excuses for his sin.

GETTING ACQUAINTED

Excuses, Excuses

What is the most effective excuse you use when you mess up something? Share it with your group.

What is the least believable excuse you have heard from anyone about why he or she messed up something? Was that person serious? Share with your group what he or she said.

DOWN FROM THE IVORY TOWER

What are people's various defenses for their sin? Share a few that either you have heard or perhaps you have actually used to excuse some sin. (You will not be asked to identify which are your defenses and which are those of other people!)

What is the basis of most of these defenses?

GAINING INSIGHT

Witness for the Prosecution

Read aloud Romans 3:9-20. Notice Paul's final accusations against all of humanity, both Jews and Gentiles. Note also the support he gives for his accusations.

⁹What shall we conclude then? Are we any better? Not at all! We have already made the charge that Jews and Gentiles alike are all under sin. ¹⁰As it is written:

"There is no one righteous, not even one;
¹¹there is no one who understands,
  no one who seeks God.
¹²All have turned away,
  they have together become worthless;
  there is no one who does good,
  not even one."
¹³"Their throats are open graves;
  their tongues practice deceit."
  "The poison of vipers is on their lips."
¹⁴"Their mouths are full of cursing and bitterness."
¹⁵"Their feet are swift to shed blood;
¹⁶ruin and misery mark their ways,
¹⁷and the way of peace they do not know."
¹⁸"There is no fear of God before their eyes."

¹⁹Now we know that whatever the Law says, it says to those who are under the Law, so that every mouth may be si-

GUILTY OR NOT GUILTY?

lenced and the whole world held accountable to God. ²⁰Therefore no one will be declared righteous in His sight by observing the Law; rather, through the Law we become conscious of sin.

Romans 3:9-20

In the space below, list the accusations that Paul makes against all of humanity in verses 9-18.

How many classes of people did the people in Rome seem to think there were in God's sight? (See v. 9.)

In verse 20, Paul states why the Law is not useful for righteousness. What is his argument?

In groups of two, try to summarize Paul's accusation in your own words.

After you and your partner have written your summary, share it with the rest of your group. What insights did others have to contribute to your perspective? Add additional ideas to your summary. What you have written in summary form is, in legal terms, God's brief as prosecuting attorney against all people.

We talked about "bad news" in the last session. Now we come to the end of the bad news. It cannot get any worse. Romans 1:18-32 seemed pretty bad, but is often dismissed by "moral people" as not about them. We have already seen, however, that this accusation is about all people—immoral and so-called "moral" ones. Outline Paul's argument from 3:9-20 that refutes the idea that there are "moral" people who have an earned righteousness.

In verses 10-18, Paul quotes from the Psalms, Ecclesiastes, and Isaiah to make his point. Isaiah 64:6 also points to only one irrefutable conclusion about the human condition.

> ⁶All of us have become like one who is unclean,
> and all our righteous acts are like filthy rags;
> we all shrivel up like a leaf,
> and like the wind our sins sweep us away.
>
> Isaiah 64:6

Write in your own words how you would describe humanity's condition based on these passages.

Put yourself in Rome listening to Paul's letter being read to you. See yourself sitting on a lounge chair or on the floor, back to the wall. Your fellowship group of Christians has just received this parchment. It is a long letter from the Apostle Paul, about whom you have heard so much recently. Eagerly you listen as a person reads aloud Paul's letter to you. How would you have felt by the time the reader got to 3:20? Depressed, hurt, angry, frustrated, or what? In just two or three words, describe how you might have felt.

GUILTY OR NOT GUILTY?

Share your "Roman feelings" with the others in your group.

Why do you think that Paul spent all this time concentrating on the bad news? What was his point in all of this?

Divide into two groups. Both groups have the same assignment: Suppose you are a reporter for the Rome Evening Television News. You have heard about Paul's accusations against all the people of the whole world and, miraculously, Paul is on the scene. You are interviewing him about all these accusations. Write three questions that you would want to ask Paul about his accusations.

Witness for the Defense
At last! Things are looking better! Read aloud Romans 3:21-31.

²¹**But now a righteousness from God, apart from Law, has been made known, to which the Law and the Prophets testify. ²²This righteousness from God comes through faith in Jesus Christ to all who believe. There is no difference, ²³for all have sinned and fall short of the glory of God, ²⁴and are justified freely by His grace through the redemption that came by Christ Jesus. ²⁵God presented Him as a sacrifice of atonement, through faith in His blood. He did this to demonstrate His justice, because in His forbearance He had left the sins committed beforehand unpunished—²⁶He did it to demonstrate His justice at the present time, so as to be just and the One who justifies those who have faith in Jesus.**

²⁷**Where, then, is boasting? It is excluded. On what principle? On that of observing the Law? No, but on that of faith. ²⁸For we maintain that a man is justified by faith apart from observing the Law. ²⁹Is God the God of Jews only? Is He not**

the God of Gentiles too? Yes, of Gentiles too, ³⁰since there is only one God, who will justify the circumcised by faith and the uncircumcised through that same faith. ³¹Do we, then, nullify the Law by this faith? Not at all! Rather, we uphold the Law.

Romans 3:21-31

What words in verse 21 contrasts it with verses 9-20? What do these words signal will happen next?

Reread silently 3:21-25. What seem to be three or four crucial phrases about the Good News in these five verses? Indicate these phrases and their verses by writing them below in the first column:

PHRASES	DEFINITION/MEANING
1.	1.
2.	2.
3.	3.
4.	4.

Why are these phrases so significant? In groups of two, try to write a brief definition of two or three of these crucial words or phrases. Write your definition in the second column above.

What is the Lord Jesus' critical role in these phrases? Describe that role in a sentence or two and share it with your entire group.

Reread verses 27-31. State in a few words the relationship of faith to all this.

Earlier you imagined yourselves as reporters questioning Paul about his accusations against humanity. Now, imagine that you are Paul. You are asked by the TV reporter to make a statement about the Good News that you have to share with the "viewers," something to cheer them up after all this really dreadful news. Write a short paragraph about the Good News. Be prepared to read it aloud to each other.

How did you feel as you heard each other's report of "Good News"? Write a few words to describe your feelings. Share them with the whole group.

GROWING BY DOING

From Definition to Action
What do justification, redemption, atonement, grace, and faith suggest to you in terms of actions that you should take or have already begun to take? List a few actions or responses that are appropriate to these words. Share these with your whole group. Add to your list.

How do all these words relate to "living by faith"? (1:17)

Check or circle at least one action that you wrote down that you feel you should take based your study of this session's passage. If you are willing, share this action with your group.

Select a family member, friend, or acquaintance to whom you could show this action during this week. Write his or her initials here.

Team up with one other person and share your anticipated actions. Commit with that person to pray and be an encourager for each other throughout this week.

Close your group session with a prayer of consecration and commitment to do what you determined.

GOING THE SECOND MILE

Encourage One Another
During the week, continue to do what you said you wanted to do based on today's study.

Call your team member from your group and encourage him or her to keep his or her commitment this week. Pray a prayer of encouragement with that person over the phone. (Prayers of encouragement are those that ask God to help others to do and be what they have committed themselves to do and be. These prayers are for the Holy Spirit's power and motivation to fulfill our commitments to the Lord.)

Part of encouragement is to communicate how well you have been doing this past week with your commitment. Being honest is the first part of communicating effectively!

FOUR

Model Students

Following the Leader

I was walking on the beach one day and noticed a boy of about eight or so taking large steps. He was attempting to follow in the tracks of a much older person who had run by him. The boy was attempting to model his stride after the older one. How much he is like all the rest of us! People are constantly casting about to find others whom they can copy—for good or ill. How many times have we heard the comment, "If so-and-so can do what he did, then why shouldn't I be able to do the same thing?" We find models who fit what we want to be and then follow them, sometimes without even thinking.

In this session, we will look at a model of faith whom we would do well to follow—not slavishly, because this model had some nasty faults. But this person's faith is a model for all of humanity since his days on earth. Paul presents him as just such a model for us to learn from.

GETTING ACQUAINTED

Heroes
Think of when you were a child and teenager.

❏ Who were your heroes and heroines? Name a few.

- [ ] Why were they your heroes and heroines?

- [ ] What did you do to mimic or model after them?

- [ ] Did you or do you still have one or two people after whom you model your faith? If you feel comfortable doing so, please share with the group either their names or their influences on you. How did they or do they influence your faith?

GAINING INSIGHT

Scripture Speaks
Read Romans 4:1-25.

¹What then shall we say that Abraham, our forefather, discovered in this matter? ²If, in fact, Abraham was justified by works, he had something to boast about—but not before God. ³What does the Scripture say? "Abraham believed God, and it was credited to him as righteousness."

⁴Now when a man works, his wages are not credited to him as a gift, but as an obligation. ⁵However, to the man who does not work but trusts God who justifies the wicked, his faith is credited as righteousness. ⁶David says the same thing when he speaks of the blessedness of the man to whom God credits righteousness apart from works:

⁷"Blessed are they
   whose transgressions are forgiven,
   whose sins are covered.
⁸Blessed is the man
   whose sin the Lord will never count against him."

⁹Is this blessedness only for the circumcised, or also for the uncircumcised? We have been saying that Abraham's faith was credited to him as righteousness. ¹⁰Under what circumstances was it credited? Was it after he was circumcised, or before? It was not after, but before! ¹¹And he received the sign of circumcision, a seal of the righteousness that he had by faith while he was still uncircumcised.

So then, he is the father of all who believe but have not been circumcised, in order that righteousness might be credited to them. [12]And he is also the father of the circumcised who not only are circumcised but who also walk in the footsteps of the faith that our father Abraham had before he was circumcised.

[13]It was not through Law that Abraham and his offspring received the promise that he would be heir of the world, but through the righteousness that comes by faith. [14]For if those who live by Law are heirs, faith has no value and the promise is worthless, [15]because Law brings wrath. And where there is no Law there is no transgression.

[16]Therefore, the promise comes by faith, so that it may be by grace and may be guaranteed to all Abraham's offspring—not only to those who are of the Law but also to those who are of the faith of Abraham. He is the father of us all. [17]As it is written: "I have made you a father of many nations." He is our father in the sight of God, in whom he believed—the God who gives life to the dead and calls things that are not as though they were.

[18]Against all hope, Abraham in hope believed and so became the father of many nations, just as it had been said to him, "So shall your offspring be." [19]Without weakening in his faith, he faced the fact that his body was as good as dead—since he was about a hundred years old—and that Sarah's womb was also dead. [20]Yet he did not waver through unbelief regarding the promise of God, but was strengthened in his faith and gave glory to God, [21]being fully persuaded that God had power to do what He had promised. [22]This is why "it was credited to him as righteousness." [23]The words "it was credited to him" were written not for him alone, [24]but also for us, to whom God will credit righteousness—for us who believe in Him who raised Jesus our Lord from the dead. [25]He was delivered over to death for our sins and was raised to life for our justification.

Romans 4:1-25

Paul argues from Abraham's faith experience to ours. Your group's task in this session is twofold. One is to analyze

Paul's argument in order to see how he develops his contention that a person lives by faith alone, apart from works and keeping the Law. The second is to reflect on Abraham's faith model and examine our own faith modeling to others.

The Great Debate
Answer the following questions individually. As soon as you finish, find two others of your group and review your answers in order to come to a basic consensus for each question. Present your findings to the entire group as if you were arguing before a group of people who thought that Abraham was justified because he obeyed God, especially God's command of circumcision. To keep things interesting, when other groups present their arguments, consider what they say in two ways. First, if you were Jews in Paul's day, how would you respond? Second, what insights do the other groups give that add to what your group of three determined? Add these additional thoughts to your own notes for each question below.

On what basis was Abraham declared righteous? See especially verses 1-5, 9-11a.

Why is it important to establish that Abraham was declared righteous prior to any good works on his part and especially prior to circumcision? (See vv. 9-17.)

How is Abraham a model for us today? (See vv. 18-25.)

What might be the role of circumcision for Abraham and for all Jews?

Give two or more reasons why faith is so important to the covenant that God made with Abraham. (See especially vv. 4-8, 13-15.)

Following Father Abraham
Graph Abraham's spiritual development as described in verses 18-21. Note some of the significant dates and events on the highs and lows.

Now, individually, in the space below draw a graph of your spiritual growth or maturity, your ups and downs.

How does your faith maturity graph compare with Abraham's?

DOWN FROM THE IVORY TOWER

As a whole group, answer this question: Why is Abraham important for us today?

As a whole group, list some of the things that you conclude it means to live by faith.

Individually, write below in a few lines what it means for you to live by faith as demonstrated by Abraham.

Read your comments aloud to the entire group. What did you learn from listening to each other's comments about living by faith?

GROWING BY DOING

Custom Model

Two major emphases are found in Romans 4. The first is that we must live by faith. Abraham modeled that for us. The second is that, just as Abraham was a model of faith, so we too are models of faith—sometimes good models, sometimes poor ones, but every day someone is probably watching and noticing how we live our faith life.

Sketch what you think your faith model looks like. Let your imagination run wild. Are you a tiger or a pussy cat, a Boeing 747 or an A1 Abrams army tank, a sharp pencil or a lined sheet of paper, a race car or a luxury car, or something else altogether? Share your drawing with your group.

Graphic Evidence
Look at your faith life. Review your graph above by asking yourself the following questions:

❏ Are you on an upward or downward slope?

❏ Regardless of whether your graph is up or down, what can you do to help your spiritual growth be more of an upward trend?

❏ Do you think that God is satisfied with the graph that you see?

❏ What can you do to make it more satisfactory to God and to you?

To the degree that you are willing, share your reflections with your group. What suggestions do you have for each other to help in spiritual growth? After all who care to have shared, pray for each other's growth.

My Audience
You are a faith model for someone. Think about those who might be looking to you as a model of Christian faith. You may not feel like a model; you may not think that your Christian life is a model of faith; you may feel very inadequate. These are not the issues. Someone is probably viewing you as some sort of model for at least some aspect of their own faith. Who is that person; who are those people? Why might they be looking to you as a model, even though you may not feel like you want to be a model? List their first names here, or use their initials.

Share with the group as much as you feel comfortable about the person(s) who look to you as a model. Listen to each other's statements. What do you hear from each other about those who look to members of your group as models?

What would you have to do to be more a more effective model? List several ideas.

Share with the group what these ideas are.

Break into groups of two and pray that each of you will be able to become a more effective model of faith this week for at least one or two people on your list.

GOING THE SECOND MILE

Pray about Your Modeling
Being a faith model this week is not easy task. You have taken on a major role. There are at least three pitfalls. One is that you will consider yourself as some sort of super-Christian, a hero of the faith, and start acting in a superior fashion. Pray for humility.

The second pitfall is that you will become somewhat preachy, a know-it-all Christian who becomes obnoxious to those around him or her. Pray for humility!

The third pitfall is that you will think *you* have to generate more faith in order to walk more by faith and to be an effective model of faith for others. God gives us faith; we do not generate it by our wills. During this whole week, pray for more faith, more of Christ, and less of self.

Now, in spite of the pitfalls, begin this week to consciously remember that people are looking at your faith model. Continue to exercise your faith in the areas of your life that need to be changed to reflect more faith.

Pray for Your Partner

Pray for your partner from your small group who is seeking to make changes in his or her life. Call each other during the week just to encourage and pray for each other even on the phone.

During this week pray for strengthened faith so that you and those in your group will become "fully persuaded that God has the power to do what He had promised." And give God the glory for your increased faith! (4:20-21)

FIVE

Peace and Joy in Life's Ups and Downs

Peace and Joy
Peace and joy! Wow! Most people would give millions of dollars if they could have either one. To have both, what would people give? No telling. Billy Graham's book *Peace with God,* published several decades ago, has been a bestseller. People want to know how to have peace, especially with God, and hopefully have joy as a side effect, too.

Martin Luther, the father of the Protestant Reformation and former Roman Catholic monk of the 16th century, sought unsuccessfully for many years to find peace with God. It eluded him until he began to study the Book of Romans. In its pages he began to realize how to receive the peace of God that rejoices in hope—regardless of the circumstances.

GETTING ACQUAINTED

Brag Books
When our daughter was born, she was the first grandchild for both of my wife's and my parents. We bought both new grandmothers a small picture album that was entitled S.O.G.W.P.I.P. What did those initials stand for? Easy: Silly Old Grandmother With Pictures In Purse. Grandmothers are expected to brag about their grandchildren, especially their very first grandchild.

We all brag a little, some more than others. What are some things that you find you might brag about? Do you brag a bit about your children, your spouse, a particularly valuable possession, a relationship that you have with someone important? In the space below, sketch a few "snapshots" that could go in your brag book. (If you have real photos with you, show them around to the group, too!)

Peace Pictures
Now think about the word peace. In the space below, draw a word-picture—a series of words or phrases—that represents peace for you.

When have you especially lacked peace about your relationship with God? If you feel comfortable, please share a little of that experience with the group.

GAINING INSIGHT

Justified through Faith
In Romans 5:1-5, Paul links peace and rejoicing (boasting) to not only the good things that go on in our lives, but also to suffering. We will see how he does this and what it all means for living by faith moment by moment.

Read Romans 5:1-5.

¹Therefore, since we have been justified through faith, we have peace with God through our Lord Jesus Christ, ²through whom we have gained access by faith into this grace in which we now stand. And we rejoice in the hope

of the glory of God. ³**Not only so but we also rejoice in our sufferings, because we know that suffering produces perseverance;** ⁴**perseverance, character; and character, hope.** ⁵**And hope does not disappoint us, because God has poured out His love into our hearts by the Holy Spirit, whom He has given us.**

Romans 5:1-5

List some words that describe what our status was before we were justified. If you need to, look back at sessions 2 and 3 for some useful insights.

Would you characterize this relationship as peaceful or alienated?

Briefly review the meaning of justification from your past sessions. Recall that justification or being declared righteous is God's act in response to our commitment in faith to Jesus Christ the Lord. He declares us "not guilty" because someone else, His Son Jesus Christ, has taken the penalty for our sins. God wipes away our sin and guilt and we stand before Him as forgiven, clean, newly born into His family. We are made just as if we had never sinned.

Paul states clearly how justification comes about. What are the key phrases in verse 1 about justification?

What has Jesus done for us? List in your own words the result of Christ's death and our faith in Him as found in verse 2.

With two others of your group, imagine that you are being introduced to God by Jesus. Role play for the group what might be your encounter. Perhaps you might say something like the following: Jesus to a new Christian, "New Believer in Me, come with Me to the throne of God. Father, I want to introduce You to New Believer. New Believer is now part of Our family. New Believer, this is the Father. Anytime you want to talk to the Father, just tell the angels that you are coming in My name and you will have direct and immediate access to Him. No one will ever stop you, ever! You will not need a priest, pastor, friend, or relative to be your intermediary. I alone will do it. Just come in My name to the Father."

Peace with God
Peace is not just the cessation of strife. It is a positive relationship that is based on a new encounter with God. We are no longer battling God; hostilities have ceased between us and God; we no longer self-centeredly seek to do our own religion; we are no longer trying to control God by making Him give us things because we obeyed His Law. Peace is a wholeness, completeness, and settledness of our relationship with God through Christ by faith.

How does "peace with God" contrast with the original relationship with God that Paul described in Romans 1:18–3:20?

In groups of two, design a two-minute demonstration of our relationship with God before and after our being justified by faith through our Lord Jesus Christ. Try to show quickly how we were before and after faith in Christ.

Joy in Hope and Suffering
Peace with God is just one of two outcomes of being justified by faith. The second outcome is stated in verses 2b and 3. The second outcome has two parts. Write the second outcome and its two parts here.

What does it mean to say, "We have hope"?

Why is hope so important in our world?

PEACE AND JOY IN LIFE'S UPS AND DOWNS

Most people have little or no problem rejoicing in hope. But rejoicing in suffering is a totally different matter. I was not too enthusiastic about having a near-fatal heart attack. I could not find the peace with God that gave me the attitude of rejoicing and bragging about my hopefulness through sufferings. Sound familiar? Why do you think Paul joined rejoicing in hope with rejoicing in sufferings? Was he some sort of masochist or sadist? Let's look at three things: hope, suffering, and the results of suffering in verses 3-5.

³Not only so but we also rejoice in our sufferings, because we know that suffering produces perseverance; ⁴perseverance, character; and character, hope. ⁵And hope does not disappoint us, because God has poured out His love into our hearts by the Holy Spirit, whom He has given us.
Romans 5:3-5

Paul does something unexpected in verse three. He states that we rejoice (or boast) in our sufferings. To say the least, most people usually do not think of suffering as a thing for which we give thanks, let alone boast or rejoice in. Share with your group any value in some suffering that you have had or that you have noticed in the lives of others.

Note how Paul connects suffering with three additional traits in verses 3-4. What are these three traits and how do they relate to each other? Draw a diagram or in any other way show the relationship of these four to each other.

Is Paul expecting us to view suffering in a stoical or masochistic manner? Or does he expect us to approach suffering in a different light? Explain.

What in verses 3-4 would suggest that Paul sees suffering as grounded in something positive that results in positive outcomes? What do the words *perseverance* and *character* mean here?

List some suggestions of what it would be like to view suffering with perseverance, character, and hope in mind. That is, how would one's view of suffering be changed?

Why is hope the final outcome of suffering?

What does hope give us in the middle of our suffering?

Paul begins verse 1 with peace with God and ends verse 5 with hope and love. Why might a person who is suffering feel cut off from God's peace and not have a sense of hope and love?

How are peace with God, hope, and love connected? Why especially does Paul introduce the idea of suffering?

GROWING BY DOING

Real-life Suffering
You have covered some extremely difficult verses, difficult not in their meaning, but in their application. It is one thing to be in a small group discussing suffering, peace, etc. It is another to be a parent whose child has just been hit by a car—or to have just been told that your spouse is leaving you and getting a divorce—or to receive a "pink slip" at work and find yourself out of a job beginning today. These and many other events cause deep sufferings and cannot be casually and cavalierly swept away.

Your task in groups of two or three is to take one suffering event, dissect it, and try to see ways in which you could help a person in a real-life suffering experience to have hope, perseverance, character, and more hope. When you have come to at least a tentative approach, be prepared to share with your entire group how you would respond to such a person. If you feel particularly creative, try role-playing the situation.

My Suffering

Now examine your own life and identify one current experience of actual suffering. What is it? You do not have to share it with the group, but you should definitely identify it for yourself. It may be a fear, a sense of anxiety, a physical illness or limitation, or whatever. Label it as "my suffering."

What changes in your perspective on suffering are necessary for you to persevere and be assured of God's peace and love? Write these down here.

In the same groups of three, pray for each other's area of suffering. If you feel comfortable sharing what the suffering is and what you need to do to change your perspective on it, share it with the others in your smaller group for particular prayer, or just pray for each other generally regarding suffering.

GOING THE SECOND MILE

Persevere!

This week there are three things for you to do in the "going the second mile."

- ❏ Keep praying for your own change in perspective regarding your suffering.

- ❏ Keep praying for the other two people in your smaller group and their need for perspective change.

- ❏ Be sensitive to sufferers with whom you come in contact during the week. Look for ways to help them understand the peace, hope, and love of God in their lives.

SIX

New Life

Misery Loves Company

You sin, I sin, we all sin. Any comfort in all this sinning? If we want company in our sin, we have plenty! Some people would like to think that they are free from all known sin, and perhaps they are. But not for long. The problem is that we all sin, even after God has justified us freely by faith through His grace. It does not take a brilliant thinker to recognize that there is something about being human that causes us to sin. The Apostle Paul knew this well, too. In Romans 6 and 8 Paul deals with the issues of reigning and dwelling in sin. We will look at these issues in the two chapters in this session and the next.

GETTING ACQUAINTED

Funerals

"The reports of my death are greatly exaggerated," said Mark Twain.

This may sound morbid, but describe a funeral. In particular, what is characteristic of all corpses?

DOWN FROM THE IVORY TOWER

You may or may not have given any thought to your own funeral, but describe a few things that you think might be appropriate for your own funeral service.

GAINING INSIGHT

Life and Death
Read Romans 6:1-14.

¹What shall we say, then? Shall we go on sinning so that grace may increase? ²By no means! We died to sin; how can we live in it any longer? ³Or don't you know that all of us who were baptized into Christ Jesus were baptized into His death? ⁴We were therefore buried with Him through baptism into death in order that, just as Christ was raised from the dead through the glory of the Father, we too may live a new life.

⁵If we have been united with Him like this in His death, we will certainly also be united with Him in His resurrection. ⁶For we know that our old self was crucified with Him so that the body of sin might be done away with, that we should no longer be slaves to sin—⁷because anyone who has died has been freed from sin.

⁸Now if we died with Christ, we believe that we will also live with Him. ⁹For we know that since Christ was raised from the dead, He cannot die again; death no longer has mastery over Him. ¹⁰The death He died, He died to sin once for all; but the life He lives, He lives to God.

¹¹In the same way, count yourselves dead to sin but alive to God in Christ Jesus. ¹²Therefore do not let sin reign in your mortal body so that you obey its evil desires. ¹³Do not offer the parts of your body to sin, as instruments of wickedness, but rather offer yourselves to God, as those who have been brought from death to life; and offer the parts of your body to Him as instruments of righteousness. ¹⁴For

NEW LIFE

sin shall not be your master, because you are not under Law, but under grace.
                                                    Romans 6:1-14

Form two smaller working groups and fill out the four columns below based on the text that you just read. Under the "Who Died" column, write the person or persons who died. Under the "Who Lives" column, write the person or persons who live and any reference to life or resurrection. Under the "Effect" columns, write the general effects of either death or life on the people involved. Not every verse will have something in each of the four sections of all the columns.

WHO DIED	EFFECT	WHO LIVES	EFFECT
v. 2			
v. 3			
v. 4			
v. 5			
v. 6			
v. 7			
v. 8			
v. 9			
v. 10			

v. 11			
v. 12			
v. 13			
v. 14			

Based on your analysis of the text above, what might be some possible themes of this section? Write down what you think and share with the group.

Verse 2 paints the picture of sin as a house that we do not have to live in any longer. Why can we move out?

What are some direct implications of moving out of sin's house?

How did we die to sin?

When did you die? That is, when was your spiritual funeral? And, more important, when was your spiritual resurrection into new life in Christ?

Half Dead?
You may be thinking that all this is fine, but your life is not consistently characterized by being dead to sin. Far from be-

ing dead to sin, your life may seem to be quite alive to sin. Cheer up. You are in good company: the saints of all ages have struggled with this problem. Even Paul finds himself torn between sin and its slavery and life in Christ and its freedom. Read Romans 7:21-25.

²¹So I find this law at work: When I want to do good, evil is right there with me. ²²For in my inner being I delight in God's Law; ²³but I see another law at work in the members of my body, waging war against the law of my mind and making me a prisoner of the law of sin at work within my members. ²⁴What a wretched man I am! Who will rescue me from this body of death? ²⁵Thanks be to God—through Jesus Christ our Lord!

So then, I myself in my mind am a slave to God's Law, but in the sinful nature a slave to the law of sin.
Romans 7:21-25

What is the problem? Suggest some reasons why people sin.

In groups of two, reread Romans 6:6-10. Write below the reasons why being crucified with Christ frees us from sin. As you do, keep in mind the characteristics of dead people.

Share you conclusions with the entire group.

What happened as a result of your death and resurrection with Christ?

It is important at this point to realize who and what died. Did sin die or did we die to sin?

How does the fact that sin did not die a partial answer to why we still struggle with sin?

What are some implications of our death to sin?

How do we keep from going back to that old sinful house and moving back in almost permanently? Or, to ask the question in another way, how do we stop being slaves to the sin to which we died? Verses 11-14 cite four major things we can and should do. Next to each action below, write an example of how you might do this in your own life.

ACTION	HOW I CAN DO THIS
"Count yourselves dead to sin but alive to God in Christ Jesus" (v. 11). "Do not let sin reign in your mortal bodies" (v. 12). "Do not offer the parts of your body to sin" (v. 13). "Offer yourselves to God" (v. 13).	

What do people do who offer themselves to sin? To God? In groups of two, show how people offer themselves to sin and to God. Use your imagination, but be discreet, especially when it comes to offering oneself to sin.

What is the reason that we do not have to obey sin any longer? See verse 14.

One final comment. Notice that the disjunctive in our Christian lives is between Christ and sin, not Christ and Satan. It is the old self contrasted with our new self. It is between life and death. The old master, sin, versus the new Master, God. Satan does not enter into the picture. Why? Because Satan has been defeated already. Since we are human, we have the old self still with us. We do not need Satan to tempt us; we are tempted by our old sinful self. That old self gets us into enough sin without Satan having to lift a finger. We give Satan too much credit and too much emphasis when we assume that he is behind all of our sin. To say, "the devil made me do it" gives Satan more credit then he deserves. What is behind our sin is our old sinful self. That old self does not need outside help to tempt us. Satan, however, is more than happy to appeal to our old sinful self.

GROWING BY DOING

Taking Action
Assemble in groups of two. By now you should have a satisfactory idea of how we can stop sinning. Let's suppose a friend comes to you distraught. He or she is very concerned about a recurrent sin. Based on your understanding of the Scripture you have studied in this session, what would you tell your friend? Write it in outline form below. Be prepared to share it with the rest of the group, too.

This session calls out for you to do something with its information. Individually, list three or more actions you think you should take based on your study in this session.

If you feel comfortable, share one or more of these with your group.

Now choose at least one of the actions that you listed to work on this week. Circle or check it on your list. In groups of three, pray for each other: that God will help each to do what he or she has checked; that sin will be overcome; that each will be able to consider himself or herself dead to sin and alive to God this week.

GOING THE SECOND MILE
Overcoming

The second mile this week is to keep on doing what you have committed to do in the session. It is one thing to state, "I want to stop this particular sin in my life." It is a whole other matter to consistently walk by faith all week long. All of us need prayer for spiritual power to "stay out of sin's house" and to be servants of our new master, God. Pray for the other two people in your final smaller group. Ask God to help them this week to do what they committed themselves to do. Pray for yourself, too, for the same thing.

Keep in mind two things as you work on overcoming sin:
1. You must consider yourself immune to that sin; you do not have to do that sin this week.
2. You must remind yourself that God is your master; therefore offer yourself to God, not to sin. When you feel like you are tempted to sin, say to yourself, "Self, I give you to God. God, You are my master. Help me to live in the newness of the resurrection life of Christ."

Call at least one of the people in your group this week and offer encouragement to them. Be prepared to fight the good fight against sin, but be aware that you fight a defeated enemy. You know sin is defeated. Now fight to win!

SEVEN

SOS

Send Help!
Person One: "Did you sin this past week?"
Person Two: "Ah, um, uh, you see it was like this, I, uh, had this little problem and I really couldn't help it. It just happened."
Person One: "Oh, I see."
Person Two: "What about you, did you sin this week?"
Person One: "Uh, well, like you, I guess things just happened. You know, I tried all week long to consider myself dead to sin and alive to God. But somehow this sin thing just isn't quite dead yet. I need more than willpower to consider myself dead to sin and alive to God."
Person Two: "Now you're talking. We need help, not just ideas to think about."

Sound familiar? If you haven't had a real conversation like this, you probably could have. We all can recognize the need to consider ourselves dead to sin, as we discovered in the last session. The problem is that we find ourselves drawn into sin. We resist, but not enough. We say no, but end up succumbing. We fight, but we are defeated. We need more than talking to ourselves to win over sin. We need more than just saying, "I am dead to sin," in order for sin's allures and our own sinful self's desires to be overcome. We need help, and we need it badly. We are not fighting a fair battle. Sin, temptation, and Satan know our weaknesses better than we do ourselves. They very insidiously and sometimes brazenly hit us at our most vulnerable points. They know our "Achilles' heel" and go right for it all the time.

We all agree. We need help. Considering ourselves dead to sin does not always work. We need something or Someone to help us in our weaknesses. Paul said it well in Romans 7:24: "What a wretched man I am! Who will rescue me from this body of death?" This is what today's session is all about. We need help and we need it in a bad way. We need to find the way to have power of sin that remains in our lives now that we no longer remain in sin. What or Who will be our power source?

GETTING ACQUAINTED
Stupid Human Tricks
What is the dumbest thing you have ever done in your lifetime? If it is not too embarrassing, and if you are willing, please share it with the group, omitting the gory details and names of innocent people!

How do we get ourselves in such embarrassing situations?

Did you ever do anything that you knew you should not be doing yet you did it anyway? Again, if it is not too embarrassing or too revealing, share it with the group.

What makes us so susceptible to doing wrong things that we know we should not do?

What can you conclude about human nature and its ability to get us into trouble?

GAINING INSIGHT

Legal Evidence
Read aloud Romans 8:1-17.

¹Therefore, there is now no condemnation for those who are in Christ Jesus, ²because through Christ Jesus the Law of the Spirit of life set me free from the law of sin and death. ³For what the Law was powerless to do in that it was weakened by the sinful nature, God did by sending His own Son in the likeness of sinful man to be a sin offering. And so He condemned sin in sinful man, ⁴in order that the righteous requirements of the Law might be fully met in us, who do not live according to the sinful nature but according to the Spirit.

⁵Those who live according to the sinful nature have their minds set on what that nature desires; but those who live in accordance with the Spirit have their minds set on what the Spirit desires. ⁶The mind of sinful man is death, but the mind controlled by the Spirit is life and peace; ⁷the sinful mind is hostile to God. It does not submit to God's Law, nor can it do so. ⁸Those controlled by the sinful nature cannot please God.

⁹You, however, are controlled not by the sinful nature but by the Spirit, if the Spirit of God lives in you. And if anyone does not have the Spirit of Christ, he does not belong to Christ. ¹⁰But if Christ is in you, your body is dead because of sin, yet your spirit is alive because of righteousness. ¹¹And if the Spirit of Him who raised Jesus from the dead is living in you, He who raised Christ from the dead will also give life to your mortal bodies through His Spirit, who lives in you.

¹²**Therefore, brothers, we have an obligation—but it is not to the sinful nature, to live according to it. ¹³For if you live according to the sinful nature, you will die; but if by the Spirit you put to death the misdeeds of the body, you will live, ¹⁴because those who are led by the Spirit of God are sons of God. ¹⁵For you did not receive a spirit that makes you a slave again to fear, but you received the Spirit of sonship. And by Him we cry, "Abba, Father." ¹⁶The Spirit Himself testifies with our spirit that we are God's children. ¹⁷Now if we are children, then we are heirs—heirs of God and co-heirs with Christ, if indeed we share in His sufferings in order that we may also share in His glory.**

Romans 8:1-17

Therefore (v. 1) is a rather important word. It states a conclusion that is based on the evidence of the last seven chapters, highlights of which we have already studied. Summarize in the space below Paul's major emphases in chapters 1–7 as they form the foundation for his *therefore* in 8:1. In groups of three, write two or three short paragraphs (or use outline form) that succinctly state his major points.

Why do you think that the statement "there is now no condemnation for those who are in Christ Jesus" is so important?

The word *condemnation* is a legal word, suggesting that Paul is again thinking of a law court. We learned that justification is a legal statement by God by which He, the righteous Judge of the universe, has declared us justified, just as if we had never sinned even though we have. He is able to do this and still remain just and true to Himself because Christ has been the atoning sacrifice for our sins. The courtroom scene continues now with a reminder that we are not condemned if we are in Christ Jesus. We have been set free! Verses 1-4 state the reason why this is so. In groups of three, imagine that you are transcribing the proceedings of a trial based on these four verses.

❏ Prosecuting attorney's argument:

❏ Christian's defense:

❏ God the Father's verdict:

Let three of your whole group role play these three persons. After they have finished, add your own ideas. It would be helpful for you to take notes during the role play and then add to those notes in the discussion afterward.

Back to Nature
Go back to the Scripture passage and underline the words "sinful nature" (also translated *flesh* in the *King James* and other versions). These words refer to that part of our humanity in which sin takes up its residence. It is that part of our being which we inherited from Adam and Eve and is passed on to each of our own offspring. It is that which constantly seeks to pull us away from God. It is where sin dwells.

Paul contrasts the old sinful nature with the new nature in which the Holy Spirit dwells. In the space below, write the contrasts between the sinful nature and the new nature of the Holy Spirit as found in verses 2-17.

SINFUL NATURE	NEW NATURE

Look over what you've written about the new nature. This column could be called "spiritual mindedness." In groups of three, write a three- or four-sentence statement that explains what it means to be "spiritually minded."

When we tried to "reckon" or "consider" ourselves dead to sin, we found that our reckoning was off. Now how does the Holy Spirit help our reckoning? What does the Holy Spirit add that we did not have before? See verses 5-11.

How are "living by faith" and "living according to the Spirit" similar? Incorporate into your thinking verses 12-17.

But we find that we still sin even with the Holy Spirit living in us. Why then do we still sin? List some reasons below.

Verse 12 suggests that we are not obligated to live according to the sinful nature but according to the Spirit. How does verse 13 show us that is possible?

How do verses 14-17 give us tremendous assurance that all this is not a gift that God will yank back from us?

The action of adoption in Roman times was a very serious thing. One's whole past was wiped away and one was given a whole new family, name, and future. The old life before adoption was as if it never existed. All that mattered was what followed the adoption. When one came into a family by adoption, one had all the rights, privileges, and inheritances of any other child of that family. For all practical purposes, the adopted child was received and viewed as a naturally born child for that adoptive family. The birth family might as well not exist anymore for that child. The old family now longer had any claims on the child, and the child had no claims on his or her birth family.

How does being spiritually minded and walking by faith overcome the reasons we sin?

GROWING BY DOING

Act It Out
This session is probably one of the most crucial studies that we have done. The issues of sin and temptation in our lives are ever present. Now that you have come to understand the basics of overcoming these, how would you go about helping others to understand the means and process by which they too can find the power to overcome temptation, their sinful nature, and sin? List four to six basic principles.

In groups of three, develop a short role play in which you instruct a person in the basics that you have learned from your study in this session. Share your demonstration with the entire group. Be sure to ask questions of each group when they have finished. And be sure to add to what you have developed in order to develop a comprehensive perspective of the answer.

Act on It
Knowing how to overcome sin by the power of the Holy Spirit is a vital and first step to the final outcome of actually overcoming sin. The issue for most of us is not knowledge but action. You have seen that we are not alone in our walk of faith. We have been invaded by the Holy Spirit. His power continually resides within us. Now we can walk in Him.

On the left hand side of this page, list some sins that a majority of Christians do with some regularity.

Now to the right of the list above, write a few major steps that Christians can do with the Holy Spirit's help to overcome these sins.

Take a few minutes to think through your own life and the struggles that you have with sin. What particular sin really gets you down? You will not be asked to share these with your group. This is really a time for self-examination and a time for you and the Holy Spirit to take a "walk" through your life. Recognize that probably everyone else in your group has at least one sin that he or she is thinking about, too. All of us are in the same boat. We know what we should do; we lack the power to do it. We readily identify with Paul's statement in 7:24: "Who will rescue me from this body of death?" We have discovered who and how.

List some practical steps that you can take to defeat your particular sin. You might be tempted to lust; then what can you do to avoid this temptation? What things do you do to feed that sin? What do you need to do to avoid it? You might be burdened with unrighteous anger. What can you do to avoid this? What steps are necessary to remove anger from your personality? You might be sinning by coveting something. What are the one or two things that you can do to disarm this sin? You may be consumed with getting more and more luxurious material possessions. What do you need to do to begin to change your spending habits? You may be totally uncaring for the poor in your city or area. What can you do to reach out to those in need?

Now, pray by yourself, asking God to give you the power to overcome this sin. Ask for reminders throughout the week that will help you to remember that it is by His Spirit that you can walk by faith and overcome sin, not by keeping the Law or by your own energy and power. Tell God you need His power and might to do this. Ask for His help, and really mean it.

After a few minutes of silent prayer, continue in prayer. This time have each person add a short prayer out loud. The group facilitator will close in prayer.

GOING THE SECOND MILE

Toward Victory

This next week will be either the most exciting week in a long time in your life or one of the most difficult ones. You will find out which it will be as you go along. Either you will find that the Spirit's power is present in your life and you can quickly slay the dragon of sin, or you will find that sin is a formidable enemy against whom you will need to fight long and hard with the full power of the Spirit. In either case, the Holy Spirit will be with you and empowering you; you will not be on your own!

Commit to pray each day for at least two people in your group. And commit to pray for yourself, too. Your prayers should focus on asking the Holy Spirit to empower each person to be victorious over sin, to help each to walk by faith in the Spirit of God, to be spiritually minded, not centered on the sinful nature. Call the other two people about mid-week just to tell them that you have been praying and will continue to pray for them. You do not have to ask questions; just remind each one that you are asking God to empower and encourage them. You will probably have times of rejoicing and times when you need encouragement to keep on trusting and walking by faith in the Spirit.

EIGHT

Never Abandoned; Always Loved

Separation Anxiety
Separation anxiety is a fairly common psychological problem that many children and some adults evidence from time to time. Children—and, to a lesser degree, adults—fear being left by a loved one. We can understand how a child who is dependent on his or her parents might have a difficult time being left with some other caregiver. Many dual working parents and single working parents have observed such anxiety in their children. Often younger children will try to please their parents in countless ways in order to try to avoid their parents' leaving them. Children also throw little temper tantrums when good behavior does not keep the parents from leaving.

Consider how Christians might feel if they thought that perhaps something or someone or God Himself would cut them off from the love of God. What if some dark power made our relationship with God disappear? What if something we did made justification null and void? What if God decided to change His mind about us and remove His Holy Spirit from us? What if God went on a fishing trip and left us alone to fend for ourselves? What if God withdrew from us because He got angry with us? What if God took a vacation? What would happen to us? What messes would occur in our lives? Would we be able to stand such separation? Can you feel the anxiety building up? Just imagine your life without God in it: no one to listen to you when you prayed; no one to hear your cries of joy or sorrow; no one to direct your path. Just you and the rest of humanity and the lonely void of the universe. There you would sit: alone, powerless, defenseless, and directionless. Feel any fear and anxiety? If not, you are superman or superwoman!

GETTING ACQUAINTED

Don't Leave Me!
Recall some event in your childhood when you felt abandoned by your parents. If it is not too traumatic, share it with the group. What happened? How did you feel? How was it resolved?

If you have children now, can you remember any times when they acted as if you were abandoning them? What did you do to help them not feel this way? Share your experiences with the group.

Have you ever felt abandoned by God? If you feel comfortable sharing your experience, please do so.

GAINING INSIGHT

Getting the Context
Our study this session will focus on Romans 8:28-39, but we must see these verses in the context of what Paul wrote immediately before them. Read aloud Romans 8:18-27.

¹⁸I consider that our present sufferings are not worth comparing with the glory that will be revealed in us. ¹⁹The cre-

ation waits in eager expectation for the sons of God to be revealed. ²⁰For the creation was subjected to frustration, not by its own choice, but by the will of the One who subjected it, in hope ²¹that the creation itself will be liberated from its bondage to decay and brought into the glorious freedom of the children of God.

²²We know that the whole creation has been groaning as in the pains of childbirth right up to the present time. ²³Not only so, but we ourselves, who have the firstfruits of the Spirit, groan inwardly as we wait eagerly for our adoption as sons, the redemption of our bodies. ²⁴For in this hope we were saved. But hope that is seen is no hope at all. Who hopes for what he already has? ²⁵But if we hope for what we do not yet have, we wait for it patiently.

²⁶In the same way, the Spirit helps us in our weakness. We do not know what we ought to pray for, but the Spirit Himself intercedes for us with groans that words cannot express. ²⁷And He who searches our hearts knows the mind of the Spirit, because the Spirit intercedes for the saints in accordance with God's will.

Romans 8:18-27

Paul acknowledges the fact that as God's children, we and all of creation experience sufferings. But—and this is important—he states that we, along with all of creation—wait eagerly in hope for the liberation from bondage to decay and death that both are suffering. We hope for "the glorious freedom of the children of God" (v. 21).

Paul also states that we have the firstfruits of the future residing in us because we have the Holy Spirit within us. The Spirit helps us in the middle of our suffering and trials. When we do not know how to pray or when we are in such terrible straits that we cannot pray, the Holy Spirit intercedes for us with prayers that cannot be expressed in human words. The Spirit does this because He knows both us and the Father and knows the will of the Father (vv. 26-27). The Spirit pours out God's love into our hearts. Read Romans 5:5: "And hope does not disappoint us, because God has poured out His love into our hearts by the Holy Spirit, whom He has given us."

Therefore, verses 18-27 give us the foundation for hope. In your own words, write what you understand this hope to be. Share your thoughts with the rest of your group. Add insights from others to your own understanding that you have written.

Sure Hope

Now we are ready to turn to verses 28-39. Read the passage aloud.

²⁸And we know that in all things God works for the good of those who love Him, who have been called according to His purpose. ²⁹For those God foreknew He also predestined to be conformed to the likeness of His Son, that He might be the firstborn among many brothers. ³⁰And those He predestined, He also called; those He called, He also justified; those He justified, He also glorified.

³¹What, then, shall we say in response to this? If God is for us, who can be against us? ³²He who did not spare His own Son, but gave Him up for us all—how will He not also, along with Him, graciously give us all things? ³³Who will bring any charge against those whom God has chosen? It is God who justifies. ³⁴Who is he that condemns? Christ Jesus, who died—more than that, who was raised to life—is at the right hand of God and is also interceding for us. ³⁵Who shall separate us from the love of Christ? Shall trouble or hardship or persecution or famine or nakedness or danger or sword? ³⁶As it is written:

"For your sake we face death all day long;
we are considered as sheep to be slaughtered."

³⁷No, in all these things we are more than conquerors through Him who loved us. ³⁸For I am convinced that neither death nor life, neither angels nor demons, neither the present nor the future, nor any powers, ³⁹neither height nor

depth, nor anything else in all creation, will be able to separate us from the love of God that is in Christ Jesus our Lord.

Romans 8:28-39

Verse 28 is the basis of the hope that Paul emphasizes in verses 18-27. Why is this so? You have read over verses 18-27 already. Now write below how these 10 verses connect with verse 28.

What difference would it make if Paul had said, "we wish," rather than "we know" in verse 28?

Notice that Paul does not say everything is good. He leaves room for suffering and evil things to happen to us. Paul is not a "Pollyanna" person who thanks God for his suffering per se, nor is Paul a masochist who enjoys sufferings. He recognizes that bad things happen to God's children. What are we to make of these bad things? What does God do to turn sorrow into joy, tears to laughter? (Psalm 126:4-6)

Rephrase, "And we know that in all things God works for the good of those who love Him." Read your restatement to the group and add insights from each other's statements to your own.

List the two conditions Paul states in verse 28. How do they help to explain what Paul has in mind?

Sovereignty vs. Free Will?

Verses 29-30 have caused countless discussions and arguments. People take sides on the sovereignty of God and the free will of man. This question and these two verses are rather theological. Although we will not be able to answer fully to everyone's satisfaction the issues that are raised by the verses, you will be able to explore their meaning and see how Paul uses them to buttress his argument in verses 31-39. What is your understanding of predestination?

One way out of the impasse between free will and sovereignty is to take another look at time, eternity, and God's place in our space-time continuum. We dwell within the confines of time and space in which things are perceived as happening sequentially: first one thing and then another; a certain cause has certain effects, and these effects can usually be predicted. History, including our own personal history, is confined to this time-space world in which we live.

God, however, does not dwell in time and space. God dwells in eternity; He began time. God inhabits the eternal present. There is neither past nor future with Him. He knows our future because our future tense is His present tense. Our past is also present tense for Him. He sees all things, knows all things, and ultimately controls all things because He is always in the present tense. If God's "time" is always present, then predestination and foreknowledge are not sequential events as they are for us. For Him they are always in the present tense.

What is Paul trying to tell us if we understand time from God's perspective as a continual present tense?

God's Purpose

Based on what you have read in verses 28-30 and in the above material, reflect on two phrases that you have studied in this session: "Called according to His purpose," and "To be conformed to the likeness of His Son." What are God's general purposes for Christians? How would you define the ultimate purposes of God for us? In groups of three, write what you understand of His purposes for us.

Verse 31 is a rhetorical question that Paul answers. In your own words, rephrase the question and the answer as found in verses 34-36.

List and explain the things and beings that Paul says can never separate us from God. Why does Paul mention these items?

We are not abandoned or forsaken. In your own words restate this conclusion.

GROWING BY DOING

Help for the Hurting

So what do all these convictions mean in our lives? Someone in your group probably knows of a Christian who has had a particularly trying time—perhaps a job loss, bankruptcy, divorce, accident, very serious illness, unexpected death in the family. How would you use Romans 8:18-39 to help this person? What comfort is there in these verses that is not merely pious talk but real understanding of God's heart and commitment for us? In groups of three, decide on one real situation that you know of and seek to construct a response to that based on these verses. When your group is finished, share how you would seek to help that other person understand God's support and encouragement through his or her very difficult situation.

Conformed to Christ
Earlier in this session, we examined why God called us. One purpose is that we might be "conformed to the likeness of His Son." Examine your own life. To what degree are you being conformed to the likeness of the Lord Jesus Christ? What things do you need the Holy Spirit to help you change? Write one thing below.

Secure in the Son
Most people have times when they feel insecure about their relationship with God. When do you feel this way? Share this with a group of three.

Using your understanding of Paul's teaching in the passage you have just studied, show how this passage can help each of you to feel secure in Christ.

 ## GOING THE SECOND MILE

Looking Back

Your group has studied some of the most theological passages of the New Testament. Many persons have avoided Romans because they thought it was too difficult to understand. They prefer the Gospel stories or some less demanding passages. You have persevered and have finished this study. But you really have just begun in many ways. You have seen the meaning of "the just shall live by faith" as it affects our initial salvation and continues to be the theme of our daily Christian walk. You have seen that hope and faith are the key components for our daily life in Christ. You have seen that we can be victorious over sin because God has given us His Spirit to empower us. You have seen that, no matter what happens to us, we are secure in Christ.

Review your life of the past eight weeks of study of Romans 1—8. What changes have you seen in your life as a result of this study? List a few below.

Have any of these changes become almost second nature now? If so, thank God for those changes.

What additional changes do you know you must have in your life? List a few below.

Now pray for the power of the Holy Spirit to enable and motivate you to make those changes. And go in peace.

DEAR SMALL GROUP LEADER:

Picture Yourself As A Leader.

List some words that describe what would excite you or scare you as a leader of your small group.

A Leader Is Not...
- ❏ a person with all the answers.
- ❏ responsible for everyone having a good time.
- ❏ someone who does all the talking.
- ❏ likely to do everything perfectly.

A Leader Is...
- ❏ someone who encourages and enables group members to discover insights and build relationships.
- ❏ a person who helps others meet their goals, enabling the group to fulfill its purpose.
- ❏ a protector to keep members from being attacked or taken advantage of.
- ❏ the person who structures group time and plans ahead.
- ❏ the facilitator who stimulates relationships and participation by asking questions.
- ❏ an affirmer, encourager, challenger.

LEADER'S GUIDE

- ❏ enthusiastic about the small group, about God's Word, and about discovering and growing.

What Is Important To Small Group Members?
- ❏ A leader who cares about them.
- ❏ Building relationships with other members.
- ❏ Seeing themselves grow.
- ❏ Belonging and having a place in the group.
- ❏ Feeling safe while being challenged.
- ❏ Having their reasons for joining a group fulfilled.

What Do You Do . . .

If nobody talks—
- ❏ Wait—show the group members you expect them to answer.
- ❏ Rephrase a question—give them time to think.
- ❏ Divide into subgroups so all participate.

If somebody talks too much—
- ❏ Avoid eye contact with him or her.
- ❏ Sit beside the person next time. It will be harder for him or her to talk sitting by the leader.
- ❏ Suggest, "Let's hear from someone else."
- ❏ Interrupt with, "Great! Anybody else?"

If people don't know the Bible—
- ❏ Print out the passage in the same translation and hand it out to save time searching for a passage.
- ❏ Use the same Bible versions and give page numbers.
- ❏ Ask enablers to sit next to those who may need encouragement in sharing.
- ❏ Begin using this book to teach them how to study; affirm their efforts.

If you have a difficult individual—
- ❏ Take control to protect the group, but recognize that exploring differences can be a learning experience.
- ❏ Sit next to that person.
- ❏ To avoid getting sidetracked or to protect another group member, you may need to interrupt, saying, "Not all of us feel that way."
- ❏ Pray for that person before the group meeting.

ONE

Living by Faith

The goal of reflection on Scripture is to bring faith and good theology to life for us today. It would be useless to study theology only for itself and not for ourselves. It would be like hiding God's Word in our hearts to get a star on our charts rather than to keep us from sinning against Him. Good theology and faith are for everyday living, not just for thinking. To be sure, we must use our minds to know God, but our minds must direct our feelings and behavior in order for us to become more like Christ in every way.

The Apostle Paul states it well in Romans 1:17: "The righteous will live by faith." We need to know what "righteous" means. We need to know what "live" means. And above all, we need to know what "by faith" means. This knowledge is not merely bookish data that we need to memorize and spew back on a test and then forget all about it. This is knowledge that leads to wisdom and action and a change of being. We cannot be merely intellectually interested in such knowledge. We are addressing life and eternal life issues. This knowledge seeks to shape our thoughts, feelings, actions, and total beings from the moment we accept it for ourselves and from then on into and throughout all eternity.

Effective theological knowledge of this sort means something for us today, tomorrow, and forever. In this study of selected

LEADER'S GUIDE

portions of Romans 1—8, we will look at some of the major theological themes of Romans. We will work to understand what the themes mean for our thinking and living today. We will affirm them for our lives as well as find means and methods to apply them to our daily living. Ultimately, we will allow God's Word to transform us to an ever increasing walk by faith in all areas of our lives by means of the Holy Spirit's working in our thinking, feeling, and actions. We will do all this in a small group setting that will be supportive of our journey to bring good theology and faith to daily life.

As **Group Leader** of this small group experience, *you* have a choice as to which elements will best fit your group, your style of leadership, and your purposes. After you examine the **Session Objectives,** select the activities under each heading with which to begin your community building.

SESSION OBJECTIVES

√ To analyze the relationship of faith to the Gospel.
√ To list several ways to "live by faith" in our own lives.
√ To practice living by faith in the coming week.

GETTING ACQUAINTED   20–30 minutes

Have a group member read aloud **Doing Theology.** Then use the following activities to help create a more comfortable, nonthreatening atmosphere for the first meeting of your small group.

Portrait of a Theologian
Some people may not have any idea of what theology is or what theologians do. Most people do have some idea that is usually neutral at best and more often negative. This opening session contrasts those feelings and ideas with what we might feel if we could speak with the Apostle Paul, who was the supreme theologian of the New Testament. Most of us would jump at the chance to talk with Paul, even though he was a "theologian." If you can help your group to make this

connection, they will be well on the road to positive attitudes towards tackling some of Paul's deep theological insights in Romans 1–8.

Optional — Role Play
If you have sufficient time, it would be fun to role play the stereotypical theologian. Divide the group into teams of three for planning and have one on each team act out what the group thinks is typical of how a theologian might speak about God to your group.

Good News
Lead the group in discussing really good news that they have heard recently. In all probability, many of the group will describe feelings of elation, joy, happiness, wanting to share the good news with others, praise to God, etc. Keep this list in mind as you lead the group through this first session, because their response to the good news of the Gospel should echo those emotions.

Optional — Faith Walk
Before you get serious about studying Romans, do the exercise below. This will take a few minutes, but it will set the stage for the remainder of Romans.

Blindfold one person and have another person lead the blindfolded person around the room. Be sure that the leader of the blindfolded person takes him or her around some obstacles such as chairs, through doorways, over chairs, etc. To increase the challenge, the one doing the leading cannot talk. He or she can only use his or her hands to lead. Allow 3 or 4 minutes of such leading. Then switch roles. Let this second person have about 3 minutes maximum. You could do this for the whole group, but you probably will not have the time.

Ask the group to describe the roles and responsibilities of the leader and the one being led. Have them reflect on how they think each person might have felt. Likely responses: the blindfolded person had to trust the leader, was scared a bit, could not completely trust the leader, was confused, couldn't sense immediately what the leader wanted him or her to do. The leader had great responsibility, needed to be careful for the blindfolded person, was unsure of himself or herself, too.

LEADER'S GUIDE

Then ask the two participants to give their feelings and thoughts while they were engaged in this little experiment. They will undoubtedly have similar comments to the group. Plus they will add the existential dimension: they actually had those thoughts and feelings. They were the blindfolded person and the leader. They knew from experience what it is to trust, to believe, to have faith in the other person's integrity and care.

GAINING INSIGHT   30–35 minutes

Faith and Gospel
Based on the faith walk, ask each member of the group to write his or her own definition of faith. Don't try to refine definitions now; you'll do that as a group near the end of the session.

Read aloud Romans 1:1-17.

Divide your group into two groups and follow the directions to reread the text and look for references to *Gospel* and *faith*. Ask each smaller group to share their observations with the whole group, taking notes from each other's observations.

Some of the major ideas that you can bring out are: The word in Greek for Gospel is *euangelion,* which means good news. The Greek word is composed of two words: *eu,* which means good or pleasant, and *angelion,* which means announcement. We get the word angel, one who announces, from the second word. The Gospel is God's good news to us. We can receive this good news by placing our trust in God's promises to forgive our sins, to cleanse us of unrighteousness, and to declare us justified or righteous in His sight. The Gospel is revealed by God. It is His good news, not ours. Its source is God, it belongs to God, and it is revealed by God. The Gospel is about Jesus Christ, His Son, and the new life that we can have in Christ. Faith is our response. We receive it gratefully without payment. Our faith in Christ allows God to declare us righteous. This is the really good news: the righteousness that we could never achieve by being good and doing all sorts of good works God gives to us graciously and freely because of our faith in His Son Jesus Christ.

❏ What is the relationship between the Gospel and faith? The Gospel is God's power for salvation and for faith living (vv. 16-17). Good News is not just for eternal life but for daily living, not just for eternity but for today and every day. We can live for God because we have a received the Gospel about Christ into ourselves. We have a new center of power and influence that comes from God and is resident in us from salvation on. It is important that your group realize that the Gospel is not just a "fire insurance policy" but a power for living now and for eternity in God's grace and empowerment.

Responding and Receiving
As you fill in the chart, draw out the following observations:

GOD'S ACTIONS	OUR RESPONSE	GOD IN US
Reveals the Gospel about Jesus	Faith: personal trust, commitment of life to God through Christ	More confidence to live daily by faith

Some may want to talk about the meaning of "righteousness." You can forestall this discussion by telling the group that this is the focus of session 5. This first session is on faith and the Gospel. By the time you all arrive at session 5, you will be in a better place to understand the concept of righteousness or justification.

Work together to refine your definition of faith. If you cannot reach a consensus in a few minutes, have people share their perspectives and use Romans 1:1-17 to analyze each person's contributions and ideas. By the time you are finished, you will probably have an adequate consensus that may differ in language but not in meaning.

Consider the following as at least a partial definition of faith: Faith is our response to God's revelation of salvation in Christ alone. Faith is our commitment to God through Christ that rejects all self-help and self-trust in one's own power to

LEADER'S GUIDE

save one's self or to please God by good works. Faith is assurance that God alone, apart from anything we can do, can and will save us. It is receiving His mercy, grace, and forgiveness through our trust in Christ Jesus the Lord. The reward of simple faith is growth in faith.

GROWING BY DOING 15–20 minutes

Faith-less vs. Faith-full
Discuss the demonstration using questions like these:
- Why it is so difficult to live by faith?
- What are some other ways each "faith-less" scenario could be changed into a "faith-full" one?
- How does God's Good News (the Gospel) enter into "living by faith" daily?

Hot Spots
Have group members complete this section privately, then share items from their lists if they feel comfortable doing so.

Close in prayer for one another.

GOING THE SECOND MILE 5 minutes

Sharing Support
Remind the group members to call each other during the week.

Optional – Closing
Close the session with a final benediction similar to this: "In Christ's name, go in the divine power of the Good News from God about Jesus Christ His Son to live this week by faith. Amen."

TWO

First the Bad News

Probably one of the least used words in our world today is sin. We just do not like the word because it conjures up all sorts of guilt. Karl Menninger, a famous American psychiatrist, wrote a book more than 20 years ago entitled *Whatever Became of Sin?* Many secular psychologists, psychiatrists, and sociologists of our recent and current history have relegated sin to ancient history or to religious zealots. Modern people do not want to be bothered by thinking that something is morally wrong. Instead, modern thinkers and leaders in behavioral sciences place blame on "society" or some segment of society. Sin is passé for modern times; what is acceptable is to blame society and having been somehow abused or deprived as a child. To say that one has sinned is to admit to being responsible for one's own actions and being guilty for moral wrongs that one has committed—clearly unacceptable for many in our time.

The Apostle Paul would not accept our modern version of wrongdoing. He lays the blame straight at the feet of each human being. The passage for this session, Romans 1:18-32, is difficult for many people in contemporary society to accept. God's wrath or justifiable anger is onerous for modern people. But sin is even more difficult to accept. To have to think that a person is responsible for his or her choices and cannot lay the blame on one's parents, teachers, school, friends, relatives, or society at large is difficult at best for many folks today. The last person they want to blame is themselves, and the last thing they want to feel is true guilt for having transgressed God's moral revelation.

Paul does not worry about people feeling guilty in this passage. There is a good reason for the guilt feelings: we are guilty of sin. No matter who or what or where one is, each is guilty of sin and deserves God's just punishment. This is the bad news. But bad news is seen only in contrast to the Good News that Paul announced in Romans 1:1-17, which you studied in the last session. Now it is time to look at why the Good News is so good. It is necessary to look at the bad news!

Your group may want to be a bit judgmental about "those heathen sinners out there" as they read Romans 1:18-32. Let them be so for a while, if that is how they feel. Before long the session will turn from looking at the godless heathen to looking at ourselves. For we are all sinners and still sin even after the new birth. Even those who believe in the possibility of sanctification in this life struggle with the issues of sin creeping, if not galloping, around in their lives from time to time. The person who says that he or she is free from all known sin usually suffers from a lapse of memory or a powerful ability to overlook some part of his or her personhood.

As you lead the group in reflection and study on this scriptural passage, try to keep them from being defensive: "I don't have any problems with sin." Recall that "If we claim we have not sinned, we make Him out to be a liar and His Word has no place in our lives" (1 John 1:10).

As **Group Leader** of this small group experience, *you* have a choice as to which elements will best fit your group, your style of leadership, and your purposes. After you examine the **Session Objectives,** select activities under each heading.

DOWN FROM THE IVORY TOWER

> **SESSION OBJECTIVES**
>
> ✓ To determine humanity's responses to God's revelation of Himself.
> ✓ To state the effects of sin on people's relationships with God, others, and themselves.
> ✓ To acknowledge and abhor humanity's sin and one's own sin.
> ✓ To ask forgiveness of one's sins and thank God for that forgiveness.
> ✓ To begin to resist sin.

GETTING ACQUAINTED   20–25 minutes

Have a group member read aloud **Bad News.** Then use the following activities to help create a comfortable, nonthreatening atmosphere.

What Have You Heard?
Share responses to the questions given.

All the News That's Fit to Print
You need some supplies for your group meeting this week. Bring, or ask others to help bring, the front sections of this week's most popular local newspaper (enough for everyone in the group to have one front page). Look at the front pages and lead the group in sharing their thoughts and experiences.

GAINING INSIGHT   30–35 minutes

Downwardly Mobile
Undoubtedly, Romans 1:18-32 must be one of the most horrible chapters in all of Scripture. In this chapter, Paul acts as the prosecuting attorney against all of humanity. He lists humanity's sins in their increasing degradation of personal relationships. His use of "God gave them over" three times (vv. 24, 26, 28) is a literary device to heighten Paul's charge against all humanity from post-Eden through today, including the most civilized persons to the most uncivilized ones. Paul makes no exceptions. We are all guilty.

LEADER'S GUIDE

Keep in mind that Paul needs to establish humanity's guilt before we can understand forgiveness. He announces the really bad news in the strongest language possible before he reiterates and explains further the meaning of the Good News that comes from God, belongs to God, is about Christ Jesus the Lord, and is for us and our salvation.

Read aloud Romans 1:18-32. Then list the sins that Paul mentions.

Ask the group how Paul increases the crescendo of God's accusations and His responses to humanity's sins. Note especially that the people suppressed the truth by their wickedness (v. 18); they knew God but did not glorify Him nor give thanks to Him (v. 21); they became futile in their thinking and their hearts were darkened (v. 21); they claimed to be wise, but became fools (v. 22); they exchanged God's glory for images of nature (v. 23); they increased sins and God gave them over to increasing sinful desires and wickedness (vv. 24, 26, 28). Each time people sinned, they moved further away from God and God moved further away from them. He let them go their own ways, obtaining the sinful pleasures that people wanted, and all the time they kept on slipping down further in their sins. They began with a refusal of the knowledge of God and ended up destroying all natural relationships between humans and totally disregarding God.

Then and Now
Before the session, gather (or ask volunteers to gather) four to six popular, secular magazines that can be cut up (such as *Time, Newsweek, US News and World Report, People, Life,* etc.), scissors, transparent tape, three or four posterboards (at least 12" x 20"—these can be made by taping together several 8 1/2" x 14" or 8 1/2" x 11" sheets of typing paper).

Pass out the popular magazines and other supplies. Ask the group to follow the directions in the learners' guide. Ask the group to read aloud the one-sentence response to the pictures of sin that they just found. (You should expect disgust and abhorrence for the sins depicted. This is a crucial response to what Paul reveals about humanity's condition before God.)

Cause and Effect

As you work through this section, discuss the following questions:

☐ What is the basic or root sin of humanity. (The root sin in Romans is not the increasing degradation of human beings. That degradation is surely there. But the main sin is a combination of rebellion against God and a desire to "do it myself," that is, to be one's own god and law, and to live independently of the Divine Creator. God's anger is just when what He has revealed about Himself has been prostituted and adulterated by humanity's refusal to accept Him and His revelation. The continual breakdown of people's moral and spiritual lives flows from these two major roots. All the sins that follow are the result of rejecting God and setting ones' selves as supreme authority. See if those in the group have determined this "big picture" of sin that is at the root of Paul's accusation and complete condemnation of humanity.)

☐ What are the connections between the three columns in the chart? (The columns show a breakdown of all human relationships. Human beings use and abuse others and themselves because they have totally disregarded God and treated Him with contempt. They worshiped what He created and not the One who created. They were blind to truth and accepted the lie [v. 25]. The more they sinned, the more they cared less for each other, themselves, and God. They destroyed all natural, wholesome relationships in order to satisfy their sinful drives. They distorted everything from creation to relationships with each other. Note, however, that the most distorted relationships are not sexual but social: read verses 28-32 where the depraved mind is demonstrated not in sexual perversions but in interpersonal, social relationships that are evil, such as gossip, slander, arrogance, etc. While the sexual sins are gross and evil, it seems that Paul wants to be sure we recognize that even "worse" sins are not sexual but the assassination of another's character and personhood.)

☐ What are some results of humanity's sins? (Verse 18 answers that: "The wrath of God is being revealed ... against all the godlessness and wickedness of men.")

LEADER'S GUIDE

- ❏ Notice the common phrase in these verses. What do you think that phrase means? ("God gave them over....." This is undoubtedly one of the greatest punishments for living people. They could have received God's blessings; now they receive His condemnation and damnation.)

- ❏ What is the progression of the sins that Paul states? (The progression is continual degradation of humanity by increasing selfishness and reckless egocentric passionate desires. Each time God "gave them over..." it was to increasingly "worse" sins, that is, sins that showed a continual disregard for human dignity and the image of God in humanity, and continual ripping away of the most personal and intimate relationships from God's purposes to satisfaction of debased passions and desires. Pure became impure, natural desires became unnatural ones, morality became immorality, righteousness became unrighteousness.)

Encourage personal reflection in the final part of this section.

GROWING BY DOING 15–20 minutes

Rate Your Reaction

In this section, you will be helping your group to recognize that, although they may not be guilty of some of the more "gross" sins of Romans 1:18-32, they are nevertheless guilty of sin. Also, the group needs to be sure to separate the sin (which they should hate and abhor) from sinners (whom God loves and for whom Christ died). It is perhaps trite, but nevertheless true, that we need to love the sinner and hate the sin. Most of us usually hate both, especially if someone has sinned against us or if someone has been involved in some sin that we consider particularly "gross" or heinous.

As you work through the questions, remember that the goal is not to get people to publicly confess their sins but to personally face some of their sins.

Examine Yourself

Be sure to lead the group members in silently identifying their own sins. Then ask what they think is the root of sin in their lives. It may help to reflect on Adam and Eve's first sin:

103

Was it eating the forbidden fruit? Disobeying God? Or taking control of their own destiny apart from God's Word? We often want to squirm off the hook, so to speak, by saying that Adam and Eve's first sin was disobedience. This is true on a secondary level, but on the primary level, Adam and Eve's rejection of God's Word and their attempt to control their own lives lie at the bottom of disobedience. They disobeyed because they did not want God to be the Lord of their lives. The root cause of sin was egocentric self-control. Adam and Eve seemed to have said: "Thank You for Your interest in us, God, but we can take care of ourselves. Just bug-off."

Respond to God
End this section by having volunteers read the prayers that they have written. Be sure that you add your and the group's affirmation to each prayer with your "Amen."

GOING THE SECOND MILE 5–10 minutes

Releasing Control
Read aloud the first paragraph of this section, then ask the group to choose partners who will commit to praying for each other this week and will call each other twice during the week.

Optional—Closing
Close this session with a short prayer of commitment and consecration.

THREE

Guilty or Not Guilty?

As a man exited church one Sunday morning, a friend passing by asked him what the sermon was about. He said the preacher preached about sin. His friend, thinking that perhaps the preacher had some juicy comments, asked him what the preacher said about sin. The man replied, "He's against it."

This is a fairly good summary of what Paul says God's view of sin is. God is against sin! We look now at Paul's final comments in Romans about sin—the bad news that he began in 1:18—and then look to see how God has provided a way out of the moral morass of sin through Jesus Christ. This portion of Scripture is a magnificent summary of the human predicament and God's loving response to it. In our study of Romans 3:9-31 we will again see God's perspective toward sin—He's against it, too! But even more, we will see how God has made it possible for the sinful one to be transformed into a righteous one.

As **Group Leader** of this small group experience, *you* have a choice as to which elements will best fit your group, your style of leadership, and your purposes. After you examine the **Session Objectives,** select activities under each heading for your study.

105

DOWN FROM THE IVORY TOWER

> **SESSION OBJECTIVES**
>
> ✓ To summarize God's indictment of humanity because of sin.
> ✓ To acknowledge that God has saved us, not we ourselves, and accept God's salvation for ourselves
> ✓ To translate faith into action in one specific way during the week.
> ✓ To support one another in walking by faith.

GETTING ACQUAINTED   20–25 minutes

Have a group member read aloud **Good and Guilty.** Then use the following activity to help create a comfortable, non-threatening atmosphere.

Excuses, Excuses
Share responses to the questions given in this section.

❑ What is the most effective excuse you use when you mess up something? (Allow sharing within the group.)

❑ What is the least believable excuse you have heard from anyone about why he or she messed up something? Was that person serious? (Allow sharing within the group.)

❑ What are people's various defenses for their sin? (Some possible answers: 1. I'm not as bad as the other guy. 2. I'm basically a good person; my good deeds outweigh my bad deeds so God will overlook my bad ones; God judges on the curve, weighing good and bad and whatever is the most, He goes with. 3. I do good works, and I'll go to heaven in spite of my occasional sins. 4. I'm special: Jewish, Protestant, Baptist, Lutheran, parents were/are Christians, I was baptized as a child, etc. 5. I really am not so bad, but if I go to hell, I'll be with my friends and we'll have a blast! (No pun intended.) 6. I deserve a little fun, I'll confess my sin and be forgiven by God. A person has to sow some wild oats, you know. Boys will be boys.)

LEADER'S GUIDE

❑ What is the basis of most of these defenses? (I'm not so bad. I do more good than evil. God can't condemn me because I do more good than bad. Good works count with God. Trying to live a good life will help us get God's favor.)

GAINING INSIGHT   30–35 minutes

Witness for the Prosecution
Read aloud the text of Romans 3:9-20.

❑ List the accusations that Paul makes against all of humanity in verses 9-18. (His final accusation is that all are equally guilty. It is not that humans have stumbled into sin. Rather, verses 10-12 state it succinctly: we have all willingly sinned and turned away from God. God has not moved away from us; we have moved away from God. Paul supports his argument by quoting several verses from the Old Testament. Not even the Law [the Ten Commandments and the Old Testament Law of Moses] could save a person. The Law never has been able to make a person righteous. Note here as well as later in this study that the Law only raises our consciousness to sin. It is powerless to help us out of our sin.)

❑ How many classes of people did the people in Rome seemed to think there were in God's sight? (It seems that Paul purposefully mentioned both Jews and Gentiles in order to assure the people of Rome, some of whom were Jews, that God did not focus His attention on ethnic background. Righteousness did not come through inheritance as a descendant of Abraham. Having genetic connections to Abraham no more made a person righteous than walking into a stable made a person a horse. Paul goes out of his way to repeat that being Jewish does not automatically include righteousness. In fact, all of chapter 2, which we will not study directly, is aimed at refuting the idea of special relationships with God because of heredity.)

❑ In verse 20, Paul states why the Law is not useful for righteousness. What is his argument? (The Law is like a searchlight that shows what is already there. The light does not produce what it shows; it merely shines on whatever is before it. So does the Law. It does not produce sin; it shows sin to be sin [see 7:7-8.]. When we lift up a rotten log from off the ground, all sorts of creepy crawly things go slithering away. Did the light that now shines on the ground produce those creepy crawly insects? Obviously not. The light merely shows us what was already there. So the Law does not make us sin. The Law merely states unequivocally what sin is. The trouble is not in the Law but in the people who fail to keep the Law of God. The Law, therefore, does not lead to righteousness. Rather it only shows us that we are lawbreakers and consequently unrighteous. No matter how hard we try, we cannot keep the whole Law of God. See James 2:10, "For whoever keeps the whole Law and yet stumbles at just one point is guilty of breaking all of it.")

❏ Outline Paul's argument from 3:9-20 that refutes the idea that there are "moral" people who have an earned righteousness. (Paul states clearly that no one, at their basic personhood does righteousness. Read Isaiah 64:6 aloud to the group "All of us have become like one who is unclean, and all our righteous acts are like filthy rags; we all shrivel up like a leaf, and like the wind our sins sweep us away.")

❏ Write in your own words how you would describe humanity's condition based on these passages. (The one irrefutable conclusion about all of humanity's condition is that all human beings are hopeless, helpless, doomed, judged by God, and damned for eternity. Not even the Law of God can save them or us!)

Ask your group to imagine themselves in Rome listening to Paul's letter to the Christians in Rome. Ask them to be aware of how they feel as these words are read to them. (At this point in the group process, you are attempting to get the group members to not only think but to respond with their feelings. They should feel really depressed by this point. Both last week and through half of this current session, they have focused on the bad news. Most people want to move on to something better, more uplifting. They are tired of bad news. If some of these feelings are mentioned in your group, accept them, then ask why the people feel that way. Often they will just be depressed by the heaping of bad news upon bad news. Good. This is exactly why Paul spent all this time on the bad news. He wanted to prepare people to listen carefully and accept the Good News. This is also the very thing that you should attempt to bring out in the next question.)

When each group has three questions ready, let each group address the questions to the other group. The other group should decide on an answer that they think Paul might have used to reply to the question. It is fine to use Scripture in Romans to respond! After one group has asked its questions, and if there is still enough time, the other group should take its turn to ask their questions of the first group. The group facilitator can act as the moderator.

Your role as group leader/facilitator in the Rome Evening Television News interview with Paul is to keep this little dramatization moving along. Do not let it get bogged down in arguments or in petty discussions. If the first group has taken more than five minutes to ask questions, call a halt to their questions and ask the second group to ask their questions. Keep the total time for these interchanges to about 10 minutes maximum.

Witness for the Defense
Read aloud Romans 3:21-31.

❑ What words in verse 21 contrast it with verses 9-20? What do these words signal will happen next? (The words are, "But now." Paul has finished his arguments against humanity. He is going to contrast the bad news with something much better. He now turns from bad news to good news.)

❑ Reread silently 3:21-25. What seem to be three or four crucial phrases about the Good News in these five verses? (These are probably the most crucial words in the verses: righteousness from God [vv. 21-22]; justification by grace [v. 24]; redemption by Jesus Christ [v. 24]; atonement through faith [v. 25].)

The meaning of each of these phrases and the key words in each phrase would take volumes to explain. Very concisely, here is what they mean.

- ❏ Righteousness and justification are the same root word. The act of declaring a person righteous or justified is a legal act. The setting for this action is the law court. God, as the Holy Judge of all the universe, declares us "not guilty" even though we are truthfully guilty; Someone else has taken punishment in our place. Justification and righteousness mean that God has declared that we have become righteous or right with Him from His viewpoint. He does not do this capriciously or willy-nilly. Faith is its foundation; grace is God's motive; salvation is the outcome; eternal life is the goal.

- ❏ Redemption (v. 24) is the buying back of humanity from their sins. Slaves were redeemed; that is, their freedom was bought and they were liberated. God redeemed Israel from Egypt; that is, He set them free from captivity to Egypt. So God redeemed us, bought us back from slavery to sin, "by Jesus Christ." Note that righteousness comes through faith in Jesus Christ (v. 22) and redemption also comes "by Christ Jesus." The setting for redemption is the slave court.

- ❏ "A sacrifice of atonement through faith in His blood" is the sacrifice of Christ through His death on the cross. The atonement is the price paid by God to liberate humanity from sin, death, and hell. The atonement finds its root in Exodus 25:17-22 and Leviticus 16:1-34. The Day of Atonement, *Yom Kippur* in Hebrew, is the day when the High Priest made an offering for the sins of Israel. He did this on only one day each year. That Day was an especially holy day and full of dread. If the atonement sacrifice was not acceptable to God, the High Priest would die in the Most Holy Place while offering the sacrifice, and the people would suffer the wrath of God on them for their sins. Christ is the atoning sacrifice that appeases God's justified wrath (Romans 1:18 ff.), wipes away our guilt, and allows God to declare us righteous. (If you have time or if the group wants to go deeper into the concept of the atonement, read Hebrews 9:1-28, which describes the Old Tes-

LEADER'S GUIDE

tament sacrifices and relates all this to Christ.) The setting for the atonement is the altar in the Most Holy Place.

❑ What is the relationship of faith to all this? (Faith is the central part of all that God has done. It is the means by which sinners accept what God has done in Christ as being for themselves. Faith is the mechanism by which we receive what God has already done for us.)

Lead your group through the interview with Paul. Ask group members to share with the whole group what they wrote. Ask them how they felt as they heard each other's report of the "Good News."

GROWING BY DOING   15–20 minutes

From Definition to Action

In your group's listing of possible actions that they could take based on the meaning of justification, redemption, atonement, grace, and faith, look for attitudes of thanksgiving, praise, wonder, marvel, surprise, etc. Also, be aware that someone in your group may never have actually received the Good News about sins forgiven by faith in Christ. Feel free to ask the group as a whole to be sure that they have accepted Christ for themselves. Recall that no one is in a privileged position with God: all have sinned and fallen short of His glory (v. 23).

❑ How do all these words relate to "living by faith"? (They all should flow from faith and lead to more faith. Restating Romans 1:17, it is by faith from beginning to end that we live. This is good news! Justification, redemption, and atonement make sense only when we have by faith accepted Jesus Christ as our own Savior and Lord. Faith is the beginning of that new life in Christ. God has made it possible through Christ's atoning sacrifice on the cross. All we need to do is to believe and receive that sacrifice as ours. Faith is the initial step and the continuous step throughout all the rest of our Christian lives.)

Work through the remainder of the activities in this section with your group.

Close the session with a prayer of consecration and commitment.

GOING THE SECOND MILE

Encourage One Another

Encourage your group to do what they have committed themselves to do during the week. As leader, you could call several to see how they are doing, too, and share how your week's commitments have progressed. Be sure to pray with each person whom you call and encourage them to do likewise with others in their group. It is rather unusual for someone to pray over the phone with us, but it is a very effective way to fellowship around God's throne when we cannot be physically present with one another.

FOUR

Model Students

Models are convenient, and everyone needs a model sometime. But models are never perfect, especially when they come to the matter of being a model for our faith. We must never fashion our lives solely on another human model, regardless of how great he or she may appear to be. As I write this, I am reminded of several very famous pastors that I knew who have been held up as models of Christian faith and virtue. They have written books and spoken at countless churches and conferences around the world. Some have even taught at Bible colleges, Christian colleges, and seminaries. Yet each of these men—they were all male—fell into various sexual sins with women in their congregations. Their faith, held up as the epitome of what a Christian faith life should be, was not the kind that others should follow.

All models have feet of clay. We need to recognize that when we begin to pattern our lives after others. There is no doubt that in our less mature years we need many models. But as we grow and develop in Christ, we need fewer human models and can pattern our lives more directly after Christ's. This is not to say, however, that we are not models for others. In fact, there is probably no Christian who has not been a model for someone. Other believers need to see how Christ is lived out in life, and they look about to see where they can find such persons. You and I are (and will) continue to be models for others, whether we like it or not. The issue is not whether or not we want to be a model for others. It is, what kind of faith model are we? And that leads to today's session in Romans 4.

As **Group Leader** of this small group experience, *you* have a choice as to which elements will best fit your group, your style of leadership, and your purposes. After you examine the **Session Objectives,** select activities under each heading for your study.

> ### SESSION OBJECTIVES
>
> √ To examine the model of saving and sustaining faith that Abraham demonstrated.
> √ To recognize ourselves as models of faith whom others follow.
> √ To identify ways to be more effective models of faith.

GETTING ACQUAINTED 20–25 minutes

Have a group member read aloud **Following the Leader.** Then use the following activity to help create a comfortable, nonthreatening atmosphere.

Heroes

Lead your group in reminiscing about the human models that they had in their childhood and adolescent years. Note the variety of models and the way that people went about trying to copy what the models did. Most of us have probably had dozens of people whom we modeled ourselves after. Give the group time to reminisce about those significant models in their earlier years. It will probably be interesting to see the various models people had as they grew up.

GAINING INSIGHT 30–35 minutes

Scripture Speaks

Read aloud Romans 4:1-25 from the Learners' Guide. It would be best for a very good oral reader to read all this aloud. Whoever does it should be asked a few days ahead to prepare to read it. Many adults do not feel real comfortable with reading aloud unprepared.

The Great Debate
Read the instructions that follow the Scripture portion. As group facilitator, your task during each group's presentation is to help the group grapple with the text and begin to see its implications for their own faith walk and faith modeling. There will undoubtedly be times in the various smaller group presentations and dialogue when you will need to interject a question or ask for clarification. It may be that you will need to encourage the group to ask questions of each other as if they were Jews and not Christians. Help them to look at what Paul said not just from a Christian perspective, but also from the perspective of a Jew, for whom Paul's comments would be very radical! Keep things progressing smoothly along by being an active facilitator, not a passive one.

❑ On what basis was Abraham declared righteous? (Abraham was justified not by works but by faith. That is, "Abraham believed God, and it was credited to him as righteousness" [v. 3]. It is crucial for Paul to establish this fact. Abraham did nothing other than to believe God's Word to him. No good works preceded Abraham's faith and caused God to choose him. Nothing in the call of Abraham nor in the life Abraham lived before his call would suggest that Abraham had earned his righteousness. See Genesis 12:1-4 for the call of Abraham by God; Genesis 15:16, 18 for the covenant with Abraham; Genesis 17:1-14, 23-27 for the sign of circumcision; Genesis 17:14-22 for the repeat of the covenant with Abraham and the promise of the son of the covenant; Genesis 21:1-7 for the birth of Isaac, the son of promise and son of the covenant between God and Abraham that was first mentioned in Genesis 12:1-4.)

❑ Why is it important to establish that Abraham was declared righteous prior to any good works on his part and especially prior to circumcision? (Abraham is the spiritual father of all who believe God and are declared righteous based on faith in God's Word. If Abraham had been justified after circumcision, it could have been argued that his justification was based on his obedient act of circumcision, and therefore God "owed" it to Abraham to declare him righteous. But Paul argues that circumcision followed justification; it did not precede it. Thus there was no reward for doing good works or even for obeying God's Law. Instead, Abraham merely affirmed for himself what God told him; he believed God. That is all! It is also important for us that Abraham believed and was justified before circumcision because Paul states that Abraham is the father of all who believe [vv. 11b-17]. Paul argues that it is by faith that all people become the children of God. Abraham is the first, the father of all who believe and are declared righteous. He is the father of all believers, Jews and Gentiles, not just Jews only.)

❑ How is Abraham a model for us today? (Abraham showed us that we are justified by faith and that we are to live each moment by faith. Note that verse 20 says that Abraham did not waver through unbelief. Instead he was strengthened in his faith because he was completely convinced that God had the power to do what He had promised.)

❑ What might be the role of the sign of circumcision for Abraham and for all Jews? (There are several roles that circumcision played for Abraham and all other Jews. Some of these were readily acknowledged by the Jews; others were often missed.
1. Circumcision reminded them that they were in the covenant between God and Abraham. They were accepted by God through faith in Him, and circumcision was the external sign of that promise to Abraham.
2. Circumcision was not just some inconsequential act done off in the corner of the room. It was a major religious experience for the family. It became a means by which the Israelites could teach their children and remind themselves about the covenant that God made with Abraham and therefore with them, too.
3. Circumcision pointed to the faith that was the basis of Abraham's justification that preceded circumcision. Righteousness by faith and the relationship with God preceded

the commandment of circumcision to Abraham. So for all Jews after Abraham, circumcision pointed to the necessity of faith and not just a physical act in order to be declared righteous. Circumcision always pointed to faith, not just to the actual act itself. Circumcision, without faith was of no value. To many Jews, however, circumcision became an end in itself rather than a sign of the true and greater end, namely, faith in God. Many Jews figured that because they had the sign, then they must have also the righteousness that went with the sign. Often they got the order reversed: because the sign was given in infancy, they thought that they had to keep the Law of God and thus would be saved. They mistook the sign for the real thing. Faith was and still is necessary, as Paul argues in this chapter.)

❏ Give two or more reasons why is faith so important to the covenant that God made with Abraham. (First, the promise of God is worthless if humanity is justified by good works and the Law. Why? Because if Abraham had been justified by the Law, then he could brag about his accomplishments, that is, he worked for it, earned it, and God owed it to him! The promised gift is not a gift if one works for it (vv. 4-5). Second, the Law does not bring life and forgiveness but wrath. The Law does not tell people how to be justified but that their actions are sinful. A policeman does not stop us on the highway to tell us that we were driving safely. The Internal Revenue Service never writes us to thank us for our annual contribution to our federal taxes. No! Policemen and the IRS talk to us when they think we have done something illegal, when we have broken a law, when we have fallen short of the law's requirements. The Law of God is like this, too. Paul states that the Law brings only wrath, not salvation.)

Following Father Abraham
Highlight the following points as you graph Abraham's spiritual maturity as found in verses 18-21:
❏ Verse 18: Abraham believed God when things seemed hopeless; he believed God's Word.
❏ Verses 19-20: he did not weaken or waver in his faith.
❏ Verse 20: God strengthened his faith. It seems that as

Abraham exercised his faith, he received more faith to believe more. His faith grew! And he gave glory to God in the process.

☐ Verse 21: Abraham was fully persuaded that God had the power to do what He promised regarding a son for Abraham. We recognize that Abraham had some rough spots along the way (see Genesis 16, where he and Sarah decided to help God out so that they could have a son). But Abraham continued to believe God when he was told that the son by Hagar was not the one of the promise.

Ask group members to graph their own faith lives and compare them with Abraham's. Some may be discouraged. If so, point out that Abraham's faith journey was not all smooth, as seen in Genesis 16. Some may realize that they have been growing slowly with ups and downs. Encourage them to keep on growing. Some may feel like they have stagnated. Ask them how they can get moving again. The issue for us today is to keep growing in our faith so that we can come to the conclusion that Abraham had in verse 21. Have the group read aloud verses 23-24: "The words 'it was credited to him' were written not for him alone, but also for us, to whom God will credit righteousness—for us who believe in Him who raised Jesus our Lord from the dead.")

☐ Why is Abraham important for us today? (The basis for God's declaring Abraham righteous is the same as for us today. God wants us to see Abraham as a model for faith for us to follow. We cannot earn justification by doing good works. The invitation from God is to receive His gracious, merciful, and loving gift of righteousness by faith alone. God initiates the action; He issues the invitation to come to Him. Without faith it is not possible to please God (Hebrews 11:6). Faith is the first requirement for a person to be declared righteous and to continue to live a righteous life (Romans 1:16-17). Also, Abraham's life is a model or sample of what faith in God produces: God is faithful and will fulfill His promises.)

☐ What does it mean to live by faith? (Faith is exclusive, excluding all other means and conditions for obtaining righteousness. Faith replaces the Law as a means of obtaining righteousness. Faith is in opposition to all other means of seeking to achieve righteousness. Faith is not a religion, it is a relationship with God through Christ. Faith stands in contrast with all religions, religious acts, good works, and pious deeds. [Someone has pointed out that all religions of the world have some requirement of good works to earn salvation and favor with their deities. Only biblical Christianity has the Good News that salvation is a free gift from God to us.] Faith demands a response of obedience, trust, commitment, and hope. Faith is tied exclusively to the Word of God in the Gospel. Faith requires us to separate ourselves from all other lords and religions. Faith causes us to live in Christ in a new way: "the just shall live by faith." Faith provides a means for us to live each day: we live by faith moment by moment.)

Depending on the time available and the depth of the comments from your group, you may want to read the following statement regarding living by faith:

What does it mean to live by faith? It means that I cannot trust in any other person or thing. I cannot trust in any act on my part nor any act by any other human being for my salvation. I cannot earn God's righteousness nor can anyone else earn it for me. I must be declared righteous by God based on His mercy and grace and my faith in His Son, Jesus Christ the Lord.

To live by faith also means something for how I live my daily life now. I cannot enter into salvation by faith and then live my life by sight and by my own decisions and will. I must live my life, moment by moment, by faith in Christ.

If I live daily, all day long, by faith, then I cannot be responsible ultimately for my future. God is the Sovereign and He is the One who controls the future, especially my future. I walk one step at a time. I do not have a large-scale map or compass. He guides and leads me step by step. He is always present, guiding, directing, moving, helping, hindering, superintending my life, opening and closing doors, convicting me, and teaching me.

Therefore, I need not worry. I can depend on Him. All nature depends on Him and so can I. I can relax in Him and believe in Him for both my eternal future salvation and my present circumstances. If I can trust Him to save me from sin and hell, I can also trust Him in whatever earthly situation I find myself.

I am not relieved of personal responsibilities. It only means that I discharge those responsibilities under His direction by faith and in full confidence that I am in Him and that He is directing me. I can rest fully persuaded and in sure confidence that He is able to keep me in every circumstance both now and forever.

This does not mean that my life will be all pleasantness and happiness. It does not mean that living by faith is going to be all success and wealth and health. It does mean, however, that whatever I do and whatever I am or become, I rest in His unchanging mercy, love, and grace. He will direct me and keep me. I am secure; in this hope and assurance I can rest confidently.

If you read the previous paragraphs to the group, ask them to respond to them. With what do they identify with in the statement?

GROWING BY DOING   15 – 20 minutes

Custom Model
Read the opening paragraph, then ask if anyone in the group does not think that he or she is a faith model for someone else. If there is, ask the group if they think that person is correct in so thinking. Chances are that the group will disagree with that person—possibly even someone in the group looks to that person for some aspect of faith.

Ask the group to sketch what they conceive their faith model to look like.

Graphic Evidence
Use the questions in this section to review the personal graphs drawn earlier.

LEADER'S GUIDE

My Audience
What kind of people look to people in your group? Spouses? Children? Neighbors? Bible study class members? Relatives? Various friends? Probably all in the group will have some people close to them who look at them as models of Christian faith. Usually these are people who know us fairly well, such as spouse, children, family, Sunday school class, etc. It would seem that it is our responsibility to be the best model possible for these people and to be consciously aware that we are being watched by others.

GOING THE SECOND MILE   5–10 minutes

Pray about Your Modeling
Read aloud or have group members read this section aloud.

Pray for Your Partner
Make sure that everyone knows whom to call this week. Encourage the group to "live by faith" so that all will see their life of faith and give glory to God!

FIVE

Peace and Joy in Life's Ups and Downs

In this session you will study Romans 5:1-5, a relatively short passage, but one that is full of insights for our understanding and more particularly for our being—our being in Christ.

As **Group Leader** of this small group experience, *you* have a choice as to which elements will best fit your group, your style of leadership, and your purposes. After you examine the **Session Objectives,** select activities under each heading for your study.

SESSION OBJECTIVES

√ To examine the relationships between faith, justification, peace with God, suffering, perseverance, character, and hope.
√ To determine what justification does for us.
√ To identify one area of suffering in our own lives in which to exercise peace, hope, perseverance, character, and rejoicing.
√ To pray for ourselves and others who suffer.

LEADER'S GUIDE

 GETTING ACQUAINTED   20–25 minutes

Have a group member read aloud **Peace and Joy.** Then use the following activities to help create a comfortable, non-threatening atmosphere.

Brag Books
Interestingly, when scholars translated Romans 5:2 in the *New International Version,* they chose to use the English word "rejoice" for the Greek word that literally means "to boast" or "to brag." The translators knew that when we brag about something really good, we are inwardly full of joy about that thing.

Peace Pictures
Ask the group members to create a word picture of peace or peacefulness. Then ask them to share and interpret it to the group. Be sure to compliment each "artist" for his or her efforts.

There is little telling what the group members will say when sharing their experiences of lack of peace with God. Anything might come out. Be sure to keep comments short and give everyone a chance to say something. Most people will probably comment on a difficult time in their lives when they felt alienated from God and lack of peace.

If there are not many who are willing to contribute, feel free to read them the following from my experience a few years ago:

Five years ago I had a near-fatal heart attack. I stopped breathing, and if an overnight guest had not been able to give me CPR, and if the paramedics had not arrived in four minutes, I would probably have died—or suffered serious brain damage. I do not remember much of those first three days following the heart attack. I do remember one thing on that first day. As I came out of a two-hour coma, my wife saw my open eyes, undoubtedly looking scared and asking searching questions like, "What happened to me?" and, "Where am I and what will happen to me?" She told me, "You had a heart attack, but you are all right now."

123

I did not feel all right. I saw the curtain of my life descending on the stage of my life — I was finished. And I had one major thought: Cynically I said, "Thanks, God, for this!" And then I added, "Where were You, God, when I needed You?"

I was definitely not at peace with God. I was angry with God. I felt betrayed, defenseless, worthless, and about to drop into the earth (if not the grave).

After you have read this to the group, ask if any of them have felt that God was far away. Ask them to share those experiences briefly.

GAINING INSIGHT   30–35 minutes

Justified through Faith
Read Romans 5:1-5 and work through the exercises given.

❏ List some words that describe what our status was before we were justified. (Wrath of God on us, all sinners, wages of sin is death, worthless, ungodly, without fear of God, hopeless, self-centered, not seeking God, enemies of God, separated from God, idolatry, etc.)

❏ Would you characterize this relationship as peaceful or alienated? (It is important for the group to recognize that all those words and phrases describe a hostile relationship between God and humanity. In fact, the statement "the wrath of God is being revealed against all the godlessness and wickedness of men" [Romans 1:18] is an accurate description of our relationship with Him.)

Briefly review the meaning of justification from your past sessions. The group members' section has a paragraph summarizing the meaning of justification. You may find it useful to read this aloud to the group.

❏ What are the key phrases in verse 1 about justification? ("Through faith" and "through our Lord Jesus Christ" are those key phrases.)

❏ What has Jesus done for us? List in your own words the result of Christ's death and our faith in Him as found in verse 2. (Christ has led us to God; He has introduced us to the Father; and through Him we have continual access to the very presence of God the Father.)

Lead your group in the role play. At the end of the role play, ask them what they felt as they were being introduced to the Father. Most people will feel awe and gratitude that they have direct access through Christ to God the Father. It might be appropriate to stop and have several short prayers of thanksgiving to God for that direct access.

Peace with God
Read aloud the opening paragraph on peace.

❏ How does "peace with God" contrast with the original relationship with God that Paul described in Romans 1:18–3:20? (It is the difference between night and day. There could be no greater contrast. We were enemies, now we are His family. We were to suffer His wrath, now we receive His love in Christ.)

Guide your group in the demonstration described here.

Joy in Hope and Suffering
Together work through the exercises in this section.

❏ Write the second outcome and its two parts here. (The second outcome is twofold. We rejoice (or boast) in the hope of the glory of God and we rejoice in our sufferings. Point out that the NIV translation of *rejoice* means literally to boast, not in a braggadocios way, but in the sense of a triumphant rejoicing in sure confidence that God will keep His Word.)
❏ What does it mean to say, "We have hope"? (We mean that something good will happen even though something bad might be occurring now.)
❏ Why is hope so important in our world? (This world is full of pain and sufferings. Things do not always go our way. The righteous suffer; the ungodly prosper; our enemies sometimes triumph over us. We ask often where God is in all of this. We realize that without hope in God, we live a futile life without much of a past and with no future except eventual death. Hope is our stake in the future: God will

perform as He has promised; on this we can depend. Hope gives us a reason for living when all around us we see decay and destruction. Hope is God's ray of light that shines in the darkness of this world. Hope is God's presence in us that says we will not be disappointed.)

❑ Share with your group any value in some suffering that you have had or that you have noticed in the lives of others. (In any group, there will be some who have had a positive experience with suffering either directly or through someone else's experiences. Be alert to the possibility that someone may bring up an entirely negative reaction to suffering. Nothing good came from what they experienced. The best way to deal with this kind of response is to allow the person to express his or her feelings and thank him or her for sharing those thoughts. Explain that Paul seeks to show the perspective on suffering as something positive and helpful. Ask the person to "hang in there" as you look at how Paul relates suffering to something positive. Then go on to the next question.)

❑ Note how Paul connects suffering with three additional traits in verses 3b-4. What are these three traits and how do they relate to each other? Draw a diagram or any other thing to show the relationship of these four to each other. (The three traits are perseverance, character, and hope. Each is a result of the one mentioned before it. One way to draw a diagram showing the relationship of these is to draw a circle showing how one leads to the other and they all end up with hope.)

❑ Is Paul expecting us to view suffering in a stoical or masochistic manner? Or does he expect us to approach suffering in a different light? Explain. (Paul is speaking of actively grasping suffering and taking hold of it to make out of it something good. It is not suffering that really counts but what it produces in us. Read Hebrews 12:2: "Let us fix our eyes on Jesus, the author and perfecter of our faith, who for the joy set before Him endured the Cross, scorning its shame, and sat down at the right hand of the throne of God." The fact that Paul begins with hope, moves to suffering, perseverance, character, and then ends up again with hope shows that he has in mind a definite approach to suffering that is not passive and definitely not masochistic.)

- ☐ What in verses 3b-4 would suggest that Paul sees suffering as grounded in something positive resulting in positive outcomes? What do the words *perseverance* and *character* mean here? (Paul sees suffering as grounded in hope, which is why he begins with hope. He also sees positive outcomes of suffering. *Perseverance* means patience, endurance, remaining steadfast. It suggests active waiting, solidity, standing tall even though things are not well. It is active endurance, not passive acceptance of suffering. *Character* literally means "triedness" or being put to the test and being found worthy. It suggests we are put into the crucible of suffering, much like gold ore is, in order to be purified and to come out refined, pure and holy. See 1 Peter 1:6-7.)
- ☐ List some suggestions of what it would be like to view suffering with perseverance, character, and hope in mind. That is, how would one's view of suffering be changed? (You are attempting to help the group change how they view suffering. Most of us look at it as something bad to be taken along with the good in our lives. Paul says that this is not the way to look at it. Suffering produces good, not just evil. Just as the seed must struggle to grow from a seed to a large tree, so we all must go through various sufferings to produce in us the endurance and triedness of character that make us into strong and committed believers in Christ. There is no growth without struggle and suffering. Ask almost any junior higher about suffering; he or she will tell you of the struggles and suffering of being an early adolescent. Remember your own early adolescent years. Most of us would rather not! They had too much suffering of various sorts. But the way to adulthood was through those sufferings.)
- ☐ Why is hope the final outcome of suffering? (Hope is the final outcome of suffering because the perseverance and character we develop confirm God's promises to us.)
- ☐ What does hope give us in the middle of our suffering? (Note especially verse 5: "And hope does not disappoint us, because God has poured out His love into our hearts by the Holy Spirit, whom He has given us.")
- ☐ Paul begins verse 1 with peace with God and ends verse 5 with hope and love. Why might a person who is suffering feel cut off from God's peace and not have a sense of hope and love? (Often we think that we have been alienated

from God when we are suffering. We feel sometimes that God has turned His back on us, that we are left alone to wallow in our various pains of body, mind, and spirit.)

❏ How are peace with God, hope, and love connected? Why especially does Paul introduce the idea of suffering? (Paul wants us to know that suffering is for a greater good and this can be understood only from within two perspectives. One is that we are at peace with God because we have been justified by faith through Jesus Christ the Lord. God's wrath will never come on us and God never leaves us. Second is that suffering leads us to endure (persevere) and to the development of character. But such endurance is not stoical, gritting of our teeth and "bearing with it." It is seen from the perspective of hope and love. God tells us in the middle of our pain, "I love you. You are not forsaken. I am with you always, even to the end of the world." To ensure that we hear these messages God has given us the Holy Spirit who speaks to us in the middle of our suffering, encouraging and strengthening us, especially the words, "I love you!" and, "I am with you!")

GROWING BY DOING   20–25 minutes

Real-life Suffering

Give each smaller group about 10 minutes to discuss one experience of suffering. Then ask them to report to the whole group what they would say to a person in that particular suffering situation. Look for application of biblical principles found in the verses studied, especially the emphasis on hope and the role of the Holy Spirit telling us that God loves us in the middle of our suffering.

My Suffering

Lead the group in examining their own lives. Ask them to write down what changes in perspectives they need. Then ask them to assemble in groups of three to pray for one another.

GOING THE SECOND MILE

Persevere!

Encourage the group to do the three things listed. Close in prayer.

SIX

New Life

Romans 1:16-17 states that God has revealed Good News to us in the Gospel. The Good News is that we are declared righteous through faith in Christ Jesus. Once that has happened, we "justified ones" are to live day-by-day by faith. It is logical therefore, to conclude that the sin that had us captured and enslaved has been broken. Whereas once we were not free not to sin, now we are free not to sin. If the Good News means anything, it must mean that sin and its grip on our lives has been broken. Otherwise, how could the news be called good? We need to be assured that what we hoped would happen when we placed our faith in Christ has indeed occurred: we have been set free from sin. We need to know this mentally and experientially. It must not be just a doctrine to be accepted but a way of life for us.

As **Group Leader** of this small group experience, *you* have a choice as to which elements will best fit your group, your style of leadership, and your purposes. After you examine the **Session Objectives,** select activities under each heading for your study.

DOWN FROM THE IVORY TOWER

SESSION OBJECTIVES

✓ To consider one's self dead to sin and alive in and to Christ.
✓ To identify ways to live as alive Christians and dead sinners.
✓ To rely on God's power for overcoming sin this week.

GETTING ACQUAINTED 20–25 minutes

Have a group member read aloud **Misery Loves Company**. Then use the following activity to help create a comfortable, nonthreatening atmosphere.

Funerals
Lead your group through the activity. Try to keep this from becoming morbid.

GAINING INSIGHT 30–35 minutes

Life and Death
Read aloud Romans 6:1-14.

Form two smaller groups to fill out the chart. Using the biblical text, your group members should not have any problem figuring out who and what goes in each column.

Review each verse with the entire group to be sure that all of the main facts were noted. If people want to talk about questions and meaning during this time, feel free to do so. Then discuss the questions that follow.

- ❏ Based on your analysis of the text, what might be some possible themes of this section? (Possible themes include: dead to sin; alive to God through Christ; freed to be alive; from death to life; living a new life.)
- ❏ Verse 2 paints the picture of sin as a house that we do not have to live in any longer. Why can we move out? (Because we are no longer viable residents of that house of

sin. We died to sin! We no longer have a "mailing address" that has sin as part of the label. Instead, Christ has invited us to be alive in His house. He has given us the ability through the Holy Spirit to move out of sin's dwelling and into Christ's holy and eternal dwelling.)

❏ What are some direct implications of moving out of sin's house? (We no longer live there. We no longer keep on receiving sin's messages at our mailbox or by phone. We do not remain, dwell, live in sin. We have been moved out. Christ called us to move to His abode. He asked us to leave all the sinful garments and furniture and books and ideas at the old house and come to His new, holy home with Him.)

❏ How did we die to sin? (When we were baptized as Christians, we showed that we were one with Christ. Just as He died on the cross, so we died. His death was our death. Just as He was raised from the dead, so we are raised to new life. His new life is ours, too. Theologians called this the spiritual identification with Christ. It means that because of our faith in Christ we are considered by God to be "in Christ" when He died and rose again. Not that we will not die physically or that we are already resurrected physically. Rather, that part of our being that was alive to sin is now dead; that part of our being that was dead to God is now alive to Him.)

❏ When did you die? That is, when was your spiritual funeral? And, more important, when was your spiritual resurrection into new life in Christ? (Ask a few in the group to share when they died and were risen with Christ. Interestingly, the Greek verb in verse 2 that is translated "we died" is in a tense that suggests a single point of action at one particular time. We do not keep on dying to sin. [This is not the dying daily that Paul talks about in 1 Corinthians 15:31.] We died to sin just as Christ died on the Cross. He died once; we died with Him once, also. We cannot go back and die all over again to sin. We are now dead to sin and alive to God in Christ.)

Half Dead?
Read the opening paragraph and the Scripture passage. Ask the group to suggest some reason why people sin. This is not "true confessions" time, so they do not have to state the

reasons they themselves sin, just why people in general sin. Of course, people in general are probably no different than all the rest of us, so whatever your group lists will probably apply to all to one degree or another. But you need not identify that a certain reason is your personal one.

List the suggestions on a writing surface for all to see. Try to determine some basic categories for the items in the list. Some categories may be: desire for pleasure, return to past sins, gave in to temptations, "weakness of the flesh," "the devil made me do it," etc.

In groups of two, reread Romans 6:6-10 and list the reasons why being crucified with Christ frees us from sin. As the group shares its conclusions, keep in mind that Paul states a theological truth: By our identification with Christ, we die to sin. Our old self died to sin's demands. We need to keep one thing in mind: Paul's analogy of our death to sin being like dying physically breaks down in reality. Analogies are always like this. They help us to understand a concept, but they are not the entire concept. There is a difference between the analogy and the thing being compared to it. Our death to sin is not a complete death, as we can all testify. The problem is that we still know the address of the old house of sin and we go back there more often than we should. We often hear sin's siren call and feel its temptations and succumb. And, if we are completely truthful, we sometimes go looking for that old house on our own. We do not need temptation; we just return to sin on our own. Indeed, we choose to sin. The good news is that we can also choose not to sin, whereas before we could not choose not to sin.

Highlight the following points as you work through the rest of this section.

❏ What happened as a result of your death and resurrection with Christ? (We became disciples of Christ, His followers; we were given a new nature—this is addressed more fully in Romans 8.)

❏ Did sin die or did we die to sin? (Sin did not die. It is alive and well, unfortunately. We are the ones who died.)

LEADER'S GUIDE

- ❑ How is the fact that sin did not die a partial answer to why we still struggle with sin? (Sin still tries to get us to succumb to its sinful desires. It is still at work in this world. Only we can keep sin from us. Given its own way, sin will seek to ensnare and envelop us.)

- ❑ What are some implications of our death to sin? (After the group has suggested a few things, you might find it helpful to read the following: We are the ones who moved out of sin's house. The old house is still there and sin still inhabits it. The issue for us is whether or not we go back to that old house and how long we stay there. Some of us visit it too frequently; others rent a room there; others lodge there almost permanently. The issue for us is the next question: How do we get out of that old sinful house and stay away?)

Work together to list specific actions in the chart provided.

Lead your group to demonstrate how people offer themselves to sin and to God. Encourage the group not to get carried away with either demonstration.

- ❑ What is the reason that we do not have to obey sin any longer? (We do not have to obey sin because "you are not under law, but under grace" [6:14]. Paul points this out in 7:4-6, too.)

Have a group member read aloud the final paragraph of this section. You may wish to refer to James 1:13-15.

GROWING BY DOING   15–20 minutes

Taking Action
Give pairs 6 or 8 minutes to write their ideas on helping a friend. Then call for their responses. Work through the rest of the section as directed.

GOING THE SECOND MILE   5–10 minutes

Overcoming
Either read or restate in your own words the directions in this section. Close with prayer.

133

SEVEN

SOS

This session is probably one of the most crucial studies that we have done. The issue of sin and temptation in our lives is ever present. In this session, you and your group members will come to understood the basics of overcoming temptation, the sinful nature, and sin.

As **Group Leader** of this small group experience, *you* have a choice as to which elements will best fit your group, your style of leadership, and your purposes. After you examine the **Session Objectives,** select activities under each heading for your study.

SESSION OBJECTIVES

√ To identify the role of the Holy Spirit in living by faith.
√ To commit to working with the Holy Spirit and not hindering Him.
√ To identify one area of one's life in which the Holy Spirit needs to work.
√ To be people of hope.

LEADER'S GUIDE

GETTING ACQUAINTED   20–25 minutes

Have two group members read aloud **Send Help!** Then use the following activity to help create a comfortable, nonthreatening atmosphere.

Stupid Human Tricks
Allow group members to share as little or as many of their personal experiences as they wish.

GAINING INSIGHT   30–35 minutes

Legal Evidence
Read aloud Romans 8:1-17. Ask your group to summarize Paul's major emphases in Romans 1–7 as they form the foundation for his "therefore" in 8:1. (Some of the major points that should be brought out are as follow:

1. God has Good News for us in the Gospel about His Son, Jesus Christ the Lord.
2. This Good News is received by faith, apart from works.
3. Faith is the way to receive God's Good News in Christ and is also the only way to live day by day.
4. The Good News is contrasted with the bad news that all have sinned and cannot save themselves.
5. We are all sinners! The really bad news is that God's wrath is on all sinners.
6. The very bad news is that we are all condemned by God, the righteous Judge of all humanity.
7. The Good News is that there is a righteousness that comes from God through faith in Jesus Christ. God loves us. God freely forgives us because Christ has been our atoning Sacrifice.
8. Abraham, the father of the Jews, had to be justified by faith and not by works or the Law.
9. Because we are justified, we have peace with God.
10. Although we suffer, we can have hope because God has given us His Spirit, who reminds us that God always loves us.
11. We are free from sin and its penalty of eternal damnation and separation from God.
12. We need to consider ourselves in Christ as dead to sin and alive to God.

These and undoubtedly a few other ways of expressing these ideas and others are the major points in the first seven chapters of Romans. One can easily see how Paul has all these major points in mind when he begins chapter 8 with the word "therefore." He wants us to realize that he has stated all his arguments and is now drawing a major conclusion.)

❏ Why do you think that the statement "there is now no condemnation for those who are in Christ Jesus" is so important? (Because some people, many perhaps, think that because they sin that God will condemn them. But Paul has already stated that God has declared us righteous. He has given us His righteousness. He will not turn around and "zap" us because we have sinned. This is the same message that Paul states in Romans 5:1: "We have peace with God through our Lord Jesus Christ." It is vitally important that we understand the importance of Paul's statement. We are freed from both sin and the Law's controls. God no longer condemns us because we are now in Christ.)

Form trios to write an imaginary transcript from a court of law. Invite one group to role play their courtroom scene.

Back to Nature
Lead the group to fill out the contrasts between the sinful nature and the new nature. The major contrasts in these 17 verses are as follow:

SINFUL NATURE	NEW NATURE
law of sin, death	free from law of sin and death
Law powerless	God's power through Christ
condemned by God	righteous in God's eyes
live according to sin	live according the Spirit
minds set on what sinful nature desires	minds set on what Spirit desires
death	life and peace
hostile to God	controlled by Spirit
slaves to fear (and sin)	children of God

❑ In groups of three, write a three- or four-sentence statement that explains what it means to be "spiritually minded." (It is having Christ's life in us, not just our own lives. Spiritual mindedness is the inner magnet, an inner spiritual compass that points to and directs our whole life's orientation to the things that are spiritual and not of the sinful nature. Spiritual mindedness is to be invaded by a powerful outside agent who sets us free from the slavery to sin, Law, and the sinful nature, and alive to follow the righteousness of God.)

❑ When we tried to "reckon" or "consider" ourselves dead to sin, we found that our reckoning was off. Now how does the Holy Spirit help our reckoning? What does the Holy Spirit add that we did not have before? (The Holy Spirit has invaded us. The Spirit is the power that we need to indeed act like people who are dead to the old sinful nature and alive to the new spiritual nature. The Spirit gives us power not to sin. He is the One who helps us to say no to the sinful desires that are still part of our being. It is the Spirit who empowers us to live a spiritually minded life.)

❑ How are "living by faith" and "living according to the Spirit" similar? (The two phrases really speak about the same thing. To live by faith is to live by the Spirit of God. We live day by day through the power of the Spirit who gives us the strength to say no to sin and yes to God's direction in our lives. The Spirit is the new Master Whom we obey; we no longer have to obey the old master of sin and the Law. Our obligation is not to the sinful nature but to the Spirit. We can choose to follow the Spirit or our sinful nature. But the power to choose the Spirit comes from the Spirit. This is the same as "living by faith" because it is not a life of sight but of faith.)

❑ Why then do we still sin? (1. We are not free from the flesh and sin's influences. 2. We often remember the pleasantness of sin, usually forgetting the consequences we paid. Sin has, no doubt, its own allurements. 3. We often stop reckoning ourselves dead to sin and that sinful nature's desires. 4. We too often think that because we have conquered sin and the sinful nature in one area that we are therefore able to be victorious in all areas. We become self-assured and ego-centered again. 5. We stop walking by faith and in the Spirit and walk in the sinful nature.)

❏ Verse 12 suggests that we are not obligated to live according to the sinful nature but according to the Spirit. How does verse 13 show us how that is possible? (The Holy Spirit is the power to put to death the misdeeds of the body, that is, of the sinful nature. We cannot crucify our sinful natures; only the Holy Spirit can do that. When we try to put to death our sinful nature, we find that it is stronger than our wills. We need something greater than ourselves. We need something greater than our sins. We need the power of God to overcome sin. God has given this power to us in the Spirit.)

❏ How do verses 14-17 give us tremendous assurance that all this is not a gift that God will yank back from us? (Paul states that if we are led along by the Spirit of God then we are children of God. He has adopted us into His family. We are co-heirs with Christ. This is tremendous! We are given the status that Christ has: a child of God! When we feel depressed, when we have failed God, when we have sinned and no longer feel worthy to be called God's child (see Luke 15:17-19), the Spirit reminds us that we are still God's children. We have been adopted by the Spirit and we cannot be lost to God, we cannot be dropped out of the family of God. We will see more of this idea in the next and final session.)

It would be well for the group to read aloud the paragraph on what adoption meant in Roman times. The adoption process was calculated to give a very strong assurance to the adopted child that he or she could never be discarded or returned to the birth parents.

❏ How does being spiritually minded and walking by faith overcome the reasons we sin? (According to Paul, we sin because we have our minds set on natural desires; we are oriented to the wrong things. We plan how to satisfy our

LEADER'S GUIDE

sinful nature, not our new nature in Christ. In contrast, the mind set on the Spirit and His desires lives in accordance with what the Spirit desires. We can choose, with the Holy Spirit's power, on what we will focus our thoughts and being. We can choose not to sin and choose to do good. We can choose the flesh or the newness of the Spirit. When we feel we are about to sin, we can ask for help from the Spirit. When we feel we are succumbing to temptations, we can ask for power over the temptation. When we are about to satisfy our sinful nature, we can ask the Spirit to help us refocus ourselves on the spiritual nature. When we know we are about to sin, we can cry for help and the Spirit of God will help us.)

GROWING BY DOING   15–20 minutes

Act It Out
Lead the group in the role play.

Act on It
Lead group members through the items in this section. Encourage them to be honest before God but not to fear that you or anyone else in the group will ask for their responses about any particular sins.

Ask the group to pray silently for two minutes. Then close in prayer.

GOING THE SECOND MILE   5–10 minutes

Toward Victory
Read aloud or summarize in your own words the material in this section. Encourage people to commit to each other for prayer. Get people to promise to pray specifically for two particular others in the group and to commit to call each other in three or four days.

EIGHT

Never Abandoned; Always Loved

Have you ever felt abandoned by God? It is a bit scary to think of and may be a bit embarrassing to admit, but most of us have had experiences when we were not so sure that God was present, or, if He was, that what was happening really mattered to Him. We all have those moments when we feel abandoned by God, family, friends, and even acquaintances. The feelings are real, no doubt. That God has abandoned us is not real. But perceptions are very difficult to overcome.

Paul has just some of these feelings in mind when he wrote the last portion of Romans 8, which is the Scripture for this final session.

As **Group Leader** of this small group experience, *you* have a choice as to which elements will best fit your group, your style of leadership, and your purposes. After you examine the **Session Objectives,** select activities under each heading for your study.

SESSION OBJECTIVES

√ To feel secure in God's sovereign love.
√ To explore the implications for God's inseparable love for our lives.
√ To relax in God's sovereignty.

LEADER'S GUIDE

GETTING ACQUAINTED   20–25 minutes

Have a group member read aloud **Separation Anxiety.** Then use the following activity to help create a comfortable, non-threatening atmosphere.

Don't Leave Me!
Allow group members to share their experiences.

GAINING INSIGHT   30–35 minutes

Getting the Context
Have group members read aloud Romans 8:18-27 and the text following it. Let people think individually about the foundation of our hope, then share their thoughts with the rest of the group. Draw out these points:

❑ Hope is central to the Christian life.

❑ The Holy Spirit gives us that hope, and reminds us that God loves us. (You might want to refer back to session 5, where your group studied Romans 5:1-5.) He is always with us in the most difficult, even seemingly impossible situations, giving us eternal hope.

❑ Throughout our lives we will face sufferings, trials, and other difficulties. Yet the Spirit is always with us, interceding for us with the Father, and helping us not to despair but to hope. We can rest assured that when the Spirit intercedes for us, it is in accordance with the will of God.

Sure Hope
Have a group member read aloud Romans 8:28-39. (It would be very effective if the person who reads this Scripture aloud does so with the feelings that are within the words. This is a very powerful passage that strikes at the heart of our deepest fears of being abandoned by God, or that someone, some power, something will separate us from God. Ask whoever will read this passage in the session to practice reading it aloud several times before the session begins. Encourage him or her to listen to the words and try to express them not as just written words on a page but as if Paul were standing there to assure your group.)

❏ Verse 28 is the basis of the hope that Paul emphasizes in verses 18-27. Why is this so? You have read over verses 18-27 already. Now write below how these 10 verses connect with verse 28. (Verses 18-27 talk about the hope that the Christian has. But Christians often wonder what is the guarantee of that hope. Could they be mistaken in their hope? Might God forget His promises? Could Christians somehow lose what they had as part of God's family? When evil comes, is there any good in it? Has God abandoned them? Is God powerless to act when calamities strike us? Do evil experiences happen to us because God is not aware of us, because He does not care, or because He is powerless to act? On what can Christians rely?)

❏ What difference would it make if Paul had said, "we wish," rather than "we know" in verse 28? (Paul is not speaking of hope as wishful thinking; it is a certainty, a faith assurance. He is so sure that he can say that he knows that the end will be for good even though the good is quite veiled in the present circumstances. By so doing, Paul signals a conclusion in his thinking: what is anticipated is guaranteed to happen. He is so sure of this that he can say, "we know" and not just, "we wish or anticipate.")

❏ List the two conditions Paul states in verse 28. How do they help to explain what Paul has in mind? (The two conditions are 1. "those who love Him" and 2. "who have been called according to His purpose." Paul is not saying that every bad thing works out well regardless of to whom it happens. Rather, he says God works out all things for the good for those who love God and whom God has called.)

Sovereignty vs. Free Will?
Read aloud the opening paragraph, then discuss how people view predestination.
❏ What is your understanding of predestination? (The verses seem to indicate that God's foreknowledge—He knows what will happen before it happens—and His predestination and calling—He chooses and causes what will happen—are active in our justification and glorification. Some people feel that predestination, foreknowledge, and calling by God eliminate all of our freedom of choice. Others say that if we have freedom of choice as human be-

LEADER'S GUIDE

ings, we place limits on God's sovereignty. Either God is free and sovereign or humans are free and make their own choices. These two perspectives have traditionally been the only two views on the subject of free will of humans and the sovereignty of God. People who support both views find their support in these two verses.)

Read over the next paragraph. If you can summarize it in your own words, please do so. Expand on the information given by referring to Exodus 3:13-14: "God said to Moses, 'I am who I am. This is what you are to say to the Israelites: "I AM has sent me to you." ' " God told Moses that His name was "I AM," that is, I always am—neither past nor future, just always "am"-ness.

What is Paul trying to tell us if we understand time from God's perspective as a continual present tense? (God foreknew us, predestined us, and called us. This has taken place in eternity— "For He chose us in Him before the creation of the world to be holy and blameless in His sight. In love He predestined us to be adopted as His sons through Jesus Christ, in accordance with His pleasure and will" [Ephesians 1:4]—and is fulfilled in our history. We cannot impose our understanding of time and sequential events on God's perspective of an eternal now. What for us occurs over years, decades, and millennia, God sees as His present now. Predestination and foreknowledge are used to describe how God views us within in our history, not His divine present tense state of being.)

God's Purpose
Form groups of three to discuss the phrases "Called according to His purpose," and "To be conformed to the likeness of His Son." General purposes could fall under the fruit of the Spirit in Galatians 5:22-23. Romans 12:1-2 also describes a "general purpose" and conformity to how Christ is. Regardless of how your group members conclude their thinking on free will and predestination, they should focus ultimately on the purpose and call of God: being made like Jesus.)

❑ Verse 31 is a rhetorical question that Paul answers. In your own words, rephrase the question and the answer as found in verses 34-36. (Question: What can we conclude from all this? Paul has stated the following: that we have hope

143

because the Holy Spirit is in us, we are the children of God, God is active in our lives even in the most difficult circumstances, God foreknew and predestined and called us, God justified and glorified us. What do all these affirmations mean for us? Answer: God is sovereign in our lives; He is on our side. God gave us His Son, so we need never think we are abandoned by Him. No one can bring any accusation against us. We are secure in God's calling on our lives.)

❑ List and explain the things and beings that Paul says can never separate us from God. Why does Paul mention these items? (He states that nothing can interfere in our relationship with God, absolutely nothing. The list of things and beings listed in these verses is intended to cover all possibilities that we might think could scuttle our relationship with God. Paul says that absolutely no thing, person, or event can pull us away from God's love. This has to be one of the most comforting things that we can know, not just mentally, but know in our hearts.)

GROWING BY DOING 15–20 minutes

Help for the Hurting
Lead your group through this section. Help them to avoid trite statements that sound too pious. Ask them to check their comments with a reality check: How would they respond in the middle of a major calamity if some friend said the same thing to them?

Conformed to Christ
Allow group members to complete this section privately.

Secure in the Son
Form threesomes to complete this section.

GOING THE SECOND MILE 5–10 minutes

Looking Back
Encourage your group to examine their lives and to commit to continuing the changes and growth that have occurred in their lives during these sessions. Close with prayer for each one to keep on walking and living day by day by faith.